ORDER
OUT OF
CHAOS

THE AUTOBIOGRAPHICAL
WORKS OF MAYA ANGELOU

DOLLY A. McPHERSON

Published by VIRAGO PRESS Limited 1991
20–23 Mandela Street, Camden Town, London NW1 0HQ

Copyright © Peter Lang Publishing, Inc., New York 1990

First published in hardback by Peter Lang Publishing, Inc.,
New York 1990

The right of Dolly A. McPherson to be identified as author of
this work has been asserted by her in accordance with the
Copyright, Designs and Patents Act 1988.

*A CIP catalogue record for this book is available from the
British Library*

Printed in Great Britain by Cox & Wyman Ltd., Reading, Berkshire

To my parents Dr. and Mrs. James Gordon McPherson,
who dreamed dreams that inspired their children
to have visions

To Maya Angelou, for the life abundantly lived and
generously shared

To my family, extended and whole

and

To the cherished memory of—

my aunt, Miss Sallie Taylor (1889–1980),
my blood brother, Wyatt Taylor McPherson (1931–
1978),
my niece, Laura Darlene McPherson (1964–1978),
my spiritual brother, Samuel Clemmons Floyd (1933–
1986)

Contents

Acknowledgments

In preparing this essay, I have been encouraged and aided by many. I am deeply indebted to my dear friend Elizabeth Phillips for her constant and loving encouragement and for her valuable reading of my book-in-progress. And I am grateful to my family for their faith in me and their encouraging support.

For their loyalty and enthusiastic responses to my work, I am most grateful to my colleagues in the English Department at Wake Forest: Nancy Cotton, Mary DeShazer, Andrew Ettin, Gillian Overing, and Robert Shorter. And I appreciate the encouragement of Doyle Fosso, Robert Lovett, Jessica Mitford, Eva Rodtwitt, Velma Watts and Emily Herring Wilson, as well as the interest of my students at Wake Forest.

At Wake Forest University, the aid of Dean Thomas Mullen and Provost Edwin Wilson, and the Research and Publication Grant awarded me by the Graduate Council, assisted significantly in manuscript preparation and publication, and I thank the University for its support of my project. My manuscript was skillfully typed by Deirdre Perry and I thank her.

I am, finally, indebted to numerous scholars and critics for their work on American autobiography, particularly Black autobiography, and for their critical assessments of Maya Angelou as an important contemporary literary voice.

Foreword

Dolly McPherson knows that readers all over the world have engaged the autobiographical genius of Maya Angelou. She knows too that we have not failed to witness the profound impact of that genius as it continues to stage, in the most contemporary terms, the oldest drama of all: the creation and recreation of a self struggling to achieve coherence amid the contradictions of desire (human nature) and custom (tradition and law). Yet McPherson also knows that our utter delight in the story of one who dares the great adventure of living, wins the chilly prize called success, and escapes its isolating tower to remain with us a traveller still, may blind us to an achievement equally stunning but not as immediately observed.

So Dolly McPherson's *Order Out of Chaos: The Autobiographical Works of Maya Angelou* accomplishes beautifully what any work of honest scholarship should. It raises implicit questions, urges us to frame them, as all the while, it plots the course to the most fruitful answers. One of the questions that McPherson's examination fields is what have been the traditions of autobiographical narrative, especially as Miss Angelou's craft has manipulated these. As we read through McPherson's succinct introduction and arrive at "An Addendum: A Conversation with Maya Angelou," which concludes the study, we recall the configurations which have historically informed the discourse of the Self: we remember the *apology* wherein the Self defends itself for "a road taken"; the *confession* wherein the Self measures itself by a higher criterion and, though finding itself lacking, discovers the glory of itself's own truth; the *memoir*, an account of the Self's experience as that has been shaped by those whom the writer has known and by the world in which the writer/Self has assumed some stage presence; the *travelogue*, the merging of the Self with the spirit of a place allowing a discovery resulting in a deeper revelation of both; the *diary* kept for multi-personal reasons, and the *journal*, the logging in of the data of flux. And, as we recall the forms that the discourse of self-portraiture has assumed, we re-read, with Dolly McPherson, the skillfully crafted design on which each of the five autobiographical volumes of Miss Angelou works.

Yet *Order Out of Chaos* invites us not only to discover the fine brushwork of autobiographical design in the *oeuvre* of Maya Angelou, but to examine that design within the framework of a national autobiography. For, in the best spirit of contemporary scholarship, Dolly McPherson suggests that we may rediscover America through its autobiographical literature. Hence, she urges us toward another question: what has been the distinguishing quality of American autobiography? And to help us answer thoughtfully, she leads us all the way back to discover, upon reflection, the many "songs of myself" which seem to characterize the national autobiographical memory. Among these, distinct themes appear: those of the prototypical immigrant, the religious conversion, the progenitive founder, the voice of a generation, or vanity fair. Yet as early as all these, we discover a voice, one of the earliest in American expressions of the Self as history, which connects us, at once, to the voice centered in McPherson's study of Maya Angelou's serial autobiography. For in the conditions and figure of silence—the mute young girl of *I Know Why The Caged Bird Sings*—we are reminded of the proto-image evoked in the 1789 narrative of Olaudah Equiano, The African (Gustavas Vassa); it is the image of the muzzled mouth of the African enslaved in the new world.

Finding the way back to speech, the struggle for literacy, equally the struggle for self-determination is the desire ar-

ticulated by the mother voice of African American autobiographical literature modulated in the narratives of self-
emancipated men and women of that descent. That voice,
since the eighteenth century—seeming now to speak in per-
petuity—has articulated the national desire: to explore the
limits of civil and personal freedom. Yet that desire, irre-
pressible, essential, powerful—the blinding force of life itself—lives caged within the contradictions of a polity who
custom and law have historically opposed its documented
statement of Self. Situating the most prodigious contemporary autobiographer at the apex of her literary traditions,
Dolly McPherson has also centered the African American
autobiography as the procreant voice in the national literature itself. *Order Out of Chaos* is a fine achievement.

Eleanor W. Traylor
Professor of English
Montgomery College
(author of the *The Humanities and Afro-
American Literary Traditions*, 1988,
and essayist on African American fiction)

Introduction

Man knows himself only insofar as he knows the world, and
becomes aware of the world only in himself, and of himself only
in it. Every new object, well observed, opens a new organ in
ourselves.

—Goethe, Maximen und Reflexionen, VI

Build therefore your own world.

—Ralph Waldo Emerson, *Nature*

There has always been the desire and effort among Black
writers to examine themselves and to articulate and celebrate those experiences and ideals that are uniquely theirs.
New World Africans, for example, from their first awareness of themselves as Americans, wished to assert the
uniqueness and importance of their experience. Black writers have tried, by the use of autobiography and, to a lesser
degree, other literary modes, to examine themselves and
articulate their findings, not only in an effort to celebrate
their unique experiences, but also to explain their situation
to that group of the society, which could, if it chose, alter
the conditions of the writers' lives. They also meant to in-
form and educate people of their own race as to their
wretched conditions, with the hope that an informed oppressed society would swell the voices of protest and hasten
the coming of a more just system. Charles Lewis Reason,
Frances Ellen Harper, and James Monroe Whitfield were

among the early voices who sang the Black consciousness in declamatory and poetic forms. Autobiographers and polemicists like Frederick Douglass, Linda Brent, Ellen and William Craft, Solomon Northup, Martin R. Delaney and David Walker, among others, hammered out prose that was designed to awaken Black men and women to their moral obligation and situation.

In the context of a particular historical period, autobiographers examine, interpret, and create the importance of their lives. Thus, autobiographers are conscious of their lives as representative of their times or as a reflection of their era, although the emphasis may be on what is distinctive about themselves rather than on what they have in common with others.[1] But, as one critic argues, the very act of writing a life down constitutes an attempt on the writer's part to justify one's life, and implicit in every act of autobiography is the judgment that the life is worth being written down.[2] Autobiography confirms that human life has meaning, that the actions of individuals count for something worth being remembered, that individuals are, in Stephen Butterfield's words, "conscious agents of time."[3] The subject of autobiographical writing is the self becoming conscious of itself in history. Hence, the main tasks of autobiography are to depict the individual in the circumstances of one's times, and to show to what extent the society stood in one's way and how the individual overcame it.[4]

Thousands of slave narratives, written by fugitive and freed slaves, sought to awaken the conscience of a nation. These early autobiographical writings, which Sterling Brown calls "literary weapons,"[5] provided moving accounts of the slave experience and became important records of the attitudes and activities of early Americans. The major impetus of these writers was the Abolitionist Movement, which needed such stories told in the words of former slaves in order to persuade the public of the inhuman and immoral conditions of slavery. In that regard, these early narratives were pressed into service as weapons against America's most peculiar institution.[6] Nevertheless, the cultural power of these writings has had the net effect of articulating a collective myth of identity and freedom, which continues to be among the central concerns of more recent Black autobiographers in America. At the common core of such important contemporary autobiographies as *Black Boy* (Richard Wright), *Notes of a Native Son* (James Baldwin), *Coming of Age in Mississippi* (Anne Moody), *The Autobiography of Malcolm X* (Malcolm X) and the serial autobiography of Maya Angelou is the urge to articulate, as if for the first time, a sensibility at once determined and precluded by history.

Although ignored by most scholars until recently, autobiography has been one of the major forums Blacks have used to share their views, to leave a record of their struggles, to inspire future generations, and to portray the individual life as an embodiment of the larger experience of Black American life. As cultural artifacts, Black autobiography reveals a continuous dialogue with the highest ideals of the land in relation to the facts of individual experience. Given their social heritage of slavery, Black writers use autobiography to blend dramatic individualization with social and moral protest. In doing so, they create and justify a connection between their individual present and the collective past. Furthermore, they demonstrate that, collectively speaking, the history of Black Americans is an intimate part of American history and is as rich a body of experience as one would find anywhere in the annals of American life.

In addition to an invariable identity with the social and cultural history of the group, Black American autobiographers consciously or unconsciously identify with the larger experience of American life in general. In spite of differences in autobiographical mode, style and vision, Black autobiographers write to define and redefine the self, to record the history of individual self-consciousness, and to discover what it was in them and their response to life that led to their present identity. Germaine Bree calls this "becoming alive to oneself through writing."[7] Hence, autobiography is a creative act in which the writer balances the past movement of life with his present sense of self. While remembering itself is a creative act and the recording and ordering of memories even more so, autobiography, at its best, involves not only mental exploration and change of attitude, but it also represents a new state of self-knowledge and a new formulation of responsibility towards the self.[8] Consciously or unconsciously, the task of the autobiographer is always to reveal the dynamics of personal growth through the interplay between past and present and the interaction of internal and external influences. Henry Nash Smith's notion of utilizing literary works to analyze the historical and cultural past and to reconstruct patterns of past behavior, attitudes and beliefs seems borne out by the Black writer's engagement with the autobiographical form.

While autobiography emanates from the writer's personal history, it is often a means to present a corrective image of social and political trends and the moral drives and spiritual needs of Black people. As such it offers scholars and other readers a privileged access to the Black experience that no other variety of writing can offer.[9] Apart from the obvious fact that most Black autobiographers write with an overwhelming sense of the social and political injustices in America, is the less obvious fact that Black autobiography is multifaceted and often an aesthetically valuable portrayal of the American self searching for and attaining increasingly higher levels of emotional and intellectual awareness of the self and the outside world. Their personal quest for self-esteem and self-affirmation, for certainty, for self-sustaining dignity, and for a sense of psychological stability in an inconstant world continues to be the basic pattern of Black autobiography.[10] This quest is as much an internal one as a physical one.

A study of the work of Maya Angelou, autobiographer and poet, shows how the writer uses autobiography to define her quest for human individuality, identifying her personal struggle with the general condition of Black Americans and claiming a representative role not only in relation to Black Americans, but also in relation to the idea of America. Thus, through a study of her work, one gains a closer access to American cultural history. I find no precedent in American letters for the role Angelou has chosen and developed for herself. That is to say, I know of no American writer who has decided to make her or his major literary and cultural contribution so predominately in autobiographical form.[11]

Through the genre of autobiography, Angelou has celebrated the richness and vitality of Southern Black life and the sense of community that persists in the face of poverty and racial prejudice, initially revealing this celebration through a portrait of life as experienced by a Black child in the Arkansas of the 1930s (*I Know Why the Caged Bird Sings*, 1970). The second delineates a young woman struggling to create an existence that provides security and love in post-World War Ii America (*Gather Together in My Name*, 1974). The third presents a young, married adult in the 1950s seeking a career in show business and experiencing her first amiable contacts with Whites (*Singin' and Swingin' and Gettin' Merry Like Christmas*, 1976). The fourth volume (*The Heart of a Woman*, 1980) shows a

wiser, more mature woman in the 1960s, examining the
roles of being a woman and a mother. In her most recent
volume, Angelou demonstrates that *All God's Children
Need Traveling Shoes* (1986) to take them beyond familiar
borders and to enable them to see and understand the world
from another's vantage point.

While the burden of this serial autobiography is essentially a recapturing of her own subjective experiences, Angelou's effort throughout her work is to describe the influences—personal as well as cultural, historical and social—
that have shaped her life. Dominant in Angelou's autobiography is the exploration of the self—the self in relationship with intimate others: the family, the community,
the world. Angelou does not recount these experiences simply because they occurred, but because they represent
stages of her spiritual growth and awareness—what one
writer calls "stages of self."[12] One of the central concerns
in this study is the exploration of the particular kind of self
and identity that emerge from Angelou's writings.

A study of Maya Angelou's autobiography is significant
not only because the autobiography offers insights into personal and group experience in America, but also because
it creates a unique place within Black autobiographical tradition, not because it is better than its formidable autobiographical predecessors, but because Angelou, throughout
her autobiographical writing, adopts a special stance in relation to the self, the community and the world. Angelou's
concerns with family and community, as well as with work
and her conceptions of herself as a human being, are echoed
throughout her autobiography. The ways in which she faces
these concerns offer instruction into the range of survival
strategies available to women in America and reveal, as
well, important insights into Black traditions and culture.

1

Autobiography as an Evocation of the Spirit

... someday somebody'll
Stand up and talk about me,
And write about me—
Black and beautiful—
And sing about me,
And put on plays about me!
I reckon it'll be
Me myself!
Yes, it'll be me.
                    —"Notes on Commercial Theatre,"
                    Selected Poems of Langston Hughes

So why do I write, torturing myself to put it down?
                    —Ralph Ellison, *Invisible Man*

I will set my ear to catch the moral of the story and tell on the
harp how I read the riddle.
                    —Psalm XLIX

Autobiography aims to celebrate and sing the self. I know
of no other autobiographer in American letters who cele-

brates and sings her life with as much verve and display of
vulnerability as Maya Angelou. Beginning with her criti-
cally acclaimed *I Know Why the Caged Bird Sings* and continuing with *Gather Together in My Name*, *Singin' and
Swingin' and Gettin' Merry Like Christmas*, *The Heart of
a Woman*, *and All God's Children Need Traveling Shoes*,
Angelou has shown how the often self-serving autobiographical form can be transformed into a strong evocation
of the human spirit.

"I should not talk so much about myself," Henry Thoreau explained in his autobiographical *Walden*, "if there
were anybody else whom I knew as well. Unfortunately, I
am confined to this theme by the narrowness of my experience. However, I, on my side require of every writer,
first or last, a simple and sincere account of his own life,
and not merely what he has heard of other men's lives; but
some such account as he would send to his kindred from
a distant land; for if he has lived sincerely, it must have
been a distant land to me."[1]

The world of Maya Angelou—beginning with her childhood in Stamps, Arkansas, and moving successively to California, New York, Europe, and Africa—is that "distant
land" in which the retrospective imagination engages experience with its historical actualities and fictive possibilities. In Angelou's autobiographical writing, the geographical spaces that she moves in and out of become the "distant
lands" that Thoreau refers to initially. However, in a second sense, this "distant land" is something other than physical space. It is the self and the peculiar individuality of the
self that is a distant land to others. It is Angelou's constant
probing into that distant land, which is the interior self, that
makes her autobiographical writing so distinct.

Angelou evokes for us a life lived with intensity, honesty,
and a remarkable combination of innocence and knowl-

edge. The sensibility at work in her autobiography is as accurately attuned to the experiences that inspired it, both factual and imaginative, as that of the most gifted American writers. By sensibility I mean what George E. Kent has called the writer's equipment for interpreting existence; those psychic, intellectual, emotional and feeling patterns that comprise the writer's characteristic response to the experiences of life.[2]

As with any corpus of high creativity, Angelou's writing is unique in ways more readily appreciated than analyzed or stated. In the best parts of her autobiographical prose, for example, Angelou uses the narrative gifts of an accomplished writer: the graphic scenes that remain in the reader's memory long after the reading; her tight-rope walk between reality and fantasy; the way that she records and alters events; the moments of decision and indecision; the authority she wields over her own life. Yet the strengths of Angelou, the autobiographer, would also include her use of language and her impeccably accurate ear for recreating voices and dialogue; her rich portraits of a wide assortment of people, including description of the rhythms of their lives and the patterns of different environments; her use of self mockery and humor as a means of achieving honesty and distance in her work and in her portraitures of the contradictory and imaginative self; and the novelistic clarity of her writing that results from the artistic tension between her recollected self and her authorial consciousness. Implicit in this awareness is the knowledge that events are not only significant in themselves, but because they also mark points of transcendence.

In an honorary degree citation presented to Angelou by Wake Forest University (Winston-Salem, North Carolina) in May 1977, the citation reads appropriately:

Maya Angelou grew up in the Deep South, a place where she

knew poverty and prejudice as well as she knew the pungent odors and protection of her grandmother's kitchen. There in Stamps, Arkansas, she heard the talk that became the music of her life. And whether it was soft-grandmother talk, or the rich metaphorical language of the Bible, or the throbbing spirituals, or the rhythms, speech patterns and imagery of the Black preacher, or the multi-layered talk between Blacks and Whites, she captured all the sounds.[3]

What Eudora Welty writes of herself in *One Writer's Beginnings* might also be said of at least one aspect of Maya Angelou's Southern legacy: "In the beginning was the Word."[4]

Speaking of the importance of language to her development as a writer and the importance of the Bible and church to her early appreciation of "the Word," Angelou has said:

I decided when I was very young to read the whole Bible and I did so twice. I loved its cadence. And in church when the minister would make the Bible come alive . . . when he would elaborate on the story—whether it was the story of the Prodigal Son or of Dry Bones in the Valley—it would go through the top of my head. I could see it. And the tonality, and the music, and the old people . . . all that. For me, it was going to the opera.[5]

For Angelou, within spirituals, gospel songs, the Bible, and the rituals of the Black church exists a celebration of the power to nurture one's creative gifts and to endure even the worst seasons of distress. Life in Stamps was, she would recall, a good life, and none of the injustices she would encounter nor the days and nights of hard work and disappointments would corrupt her vitality nor lessen her will to survive.

"All of my work, my life, everything I do is about survival, not just bare, awful, plodding survival, but survival with grace and faith. While one may encounter many defeats, one must not be defeated. In fact the encountering may be the very experience which creates the vitality and the power to endure."[6] Angelou regards the pain she has suffered on her journey to full selfhood as an inescapable effect of growth everyone must endure. She can confront the memories of her own past because they form a necessary part of her development, and out of this acceptance emerges one of the basic themes in her work: the refusal of the human spirit to be subdued.

But how does the autobiographer transform something as private and unique as self into something that is universal? Or, in Emerson's terms, how does one adjust the angle of vision between soul and nature to express both that which is private and that which is universal?

The chronology of works in an autobiographer's canon may have everything or nothing to do with the ordering of his or her perception. Yet one may assume, and rather accurately, I believe, that an autobiographer, like every other writer, operates from a set of basic assumptions about the nature of life and of people. Both the autobiographer's self-image and image of the universe arise from these assumptions, which are fashioned by his or her experience and observations. If one examines an autobiographer's work perceptively, one can detect a pattern that reveals the writer's basic assumptions which often manifest themselves as recurrent themes in his or her work.[7] Thus through close study of the autobiography of Maya Angelou, it is possible to isolate certain nascent themes initially introduced in *I Know Why the Caged Bird Sings* and developed throughout the later volumes of her autobiography.

Angelou is not the only Black autobiographer who has focused on childhood years in the Deep South, and the painful memories of those years. Richard Wright's life, as recaptured in *Black Boy* (1945), was an unbelievable round of hunger, poverty, brutality and mistreatment. In the recollection of his childhood, he emphasized his most painful remembered experiences. Approximately a quarter of a century later, Anne Moody in *Coming of Age in Mississippi* (1968), followed a similar pattern when she brought to life, in graphic moving language, the sights and smells and suffering of rural poverty, the effort her parents made to hold a family together under pressures that were not of their own making, and her own simultaneous discovery of sexual power and social powerlessness. In sharp contrast, however, Maya Angelou is less concerned with recapturing the external conditions of her environment. While *I Know Why the Caged Bird Sings* is set in the Black community of the rural Deep South, for Angelou the Black community is more than place or setting. As an autobiographer, she is concerned with recapturing her growing awareness of her environment—her response to that environment and to the people who made up that environment: their manners, talk, gestures of bravado, their thoughts and dreams. Even though frustration and tragedy touch their lives, they retain, nevertheless, a measure of spiritual integrity.

The central themes to be culled from *I Know Why the Caged Bird Sings* and that recur throughout the autobiography are courage, perseverance, the persistence or renewal of innocence against overwhelming obstacles, and the often difficult process of attaining selfhood. Related to these is the theme of survival. By survival, I mean the largely unconscious process of creating for one's self a particular pattern of living that allows one to cope with and transcend one's particular environment in order to achieve some measure of personal worth.

Three common American autobiographical themes appear and converge in Maya Angelou's autobiographical writing: community, family and the individual. To a remarkable extent, Angelou comes full circle with these themes in the five volumes of her personal history and by the time she writes *All God's Children Need Travelling Shoes*, each thematic idea is sufficiently permutated as to represent something new for Angelou: both community and family get absolved by the individual.

In its earliest expression, community is a place, Stamps, Arkansas, whose set of traditional values is generously laced with precepts from the slave past on the matter of survival in a hostile environment. When at times the larger community threatens to be treacherous, Grandmother Henderson, the adult upon whom Angelou is directly dependent, remains uncompromising in her support and protection, nurturing and sustaining the child with her love. Thus, in *I Know Why the Caged Bird Sings*, personal values become synonymous with Stamps' communal values. However, in the mature Angelou, community is transformed into something less specific and comes to represent a community of interests which, while not devoid of all traditional Black values, is more fluid, more open to possibility and improvisation than the former. As one probes the serial autobiography, one continues to be aware of the changing definitions of community.

In Stamps, the community nurtures its members and is a force in the lives of Black people, despite the poverty of the community. Indeed, there are numerous examples that illustrate the communal character of life there, including the help that people readily give to one another. Later in St. Louis and California, Angelou lives a life which, as described, is quite isolated, and her relationships are casual and ephemeral. In this environment, she is forced into the realization that the old modes of behavior that Grandmother Henderson has insisted upon are no longer valid.

The concern for her personal growth in relation to community is most consciously articulated in *I Know Why the Caged Bird Sings* and *Gather Together in My Name*. The mature autobiographer, looking back on her childhood and adolescence, has no doubt about her connection to the community and defines herself, sometimes against, but always because of, the group identity that provides her frame of reference. The interplay between Angelou, the individual, and the group is neither so rigidly structured that her individual experience is stifled, nor so casual that she can forget that her roots are placed firmly within the group.[8]

Angelou's development of the theme, *family*, begins in a preoccupation with the traditional nuclear family (i.e., husband, wife, and dependent children), but because of her and her brother's displacement in *I Know Why the Caged Bird Sings*, the family configuration is progressively defined by Angelou's nebulous relationship to her parents, by her special relationship to her grandmother and brother, and by the tension between parents and children. Nonetheless, it is interesting to witness how the concept of family evolves beyond the extended family into a network of relationships in which trust is the key to a display of kinship concerns. The term "extended family" may be defined as a multigenerational, interdependent group which is bonded together by a strong sense of obligation to relatives; is organized around a family focused household; is generally guided by a family head or dominant family figure; and extends across geographical boundaries to connect family units to an extended family network.[9] While this permutation does not eliminate or negate the biological kinship system, it does allow for the series of "life lines" (i.e., a teacher and others) that become so important in Angelou's development. It provides as well for the cautious manner in which Angelou monitors her own relationship with her son. For example, one witnesses the way in which Angelou becomes all the forms of family for her child and thus provides him with the security she has craved. One is struck by the sharp parallels in Angelou's account of her son's developing independence and her own. Despite the concern for family, escape or migration from home and family is a recurrent pattern in Angelou's autobiography.

The individual is, of course, the essential base from which an autobiographer builds relationships to community and family. Throughout Angelou's autobiography, one finds variations on the common theme of interplay between the individual and the group. Central to this configuration is the discovery that the individual self is really a series of selves evolving around a core of values, opportunities, and experiences. Indeed, one can identify situations in *I Know Why the Caged Bird Sings* that foreshadow the evolving elements of Angelou's later "self." There is, for example, Mrs. Flowers' acceptance and encouragement that allow the child to experience the reality and power of her own worth. Another motif is naming, what Angelou is called and what she calls herself, as in her confrontation with Mrs. Cullinan, who fails to address her by her proper name, which is for Angelou already the symbol of her tentative uniqueness. Equally revealing as thematic pattern is the series of incidents in which she is shocked by acts of injustice and into an awareness of her racial identity, as in the late night visit of the Ku Klux Klan, the poor white children who disrespect Grandmother Henderson, the trip to the dentist, the graduation speech, the Joe Louis/Carnera fight; and, in a different direction, the maturity that emanates from her one-month sojourn amongst a group of homeless children in a San Diego junkyard. It is of interest to note how Angelou responds to crisis in the earlier works and to analyze how she maintains the inner core of her "self" in the midst of the constantly changing circumstances of her life.

Using Erik Erikson's definition, "crisis" in the autobiography does not always involve a catastrophe or an insurmountable obstacle but rather a "necessary turning point."[10] When, at various stages in her life cycle, Angelou realizes that old modes of behavior will no longer suffice, she recognizes that if she is to grow and develop she must find "a new way of behaving." In *I Know Why the Caged Bird Sings*, Angelou's initial crisis centers on her childhood identity—her acceptance of herself as an outcast (because of her rejection by her parents), and how she must repudiate her idealism in order to free herself from others' control. Unlike Wright and Moody, Maya Angelou does not simply break away from or reject her past; rather, like Maxine Hong Kingston, she wrestles with it, defining herself through her participation in, as well as separation from, that past. In Angelou, crisis is clearly a crucial forward step, a crucial experience that shapes her identity.

Angelou's autobiography does not shout its themes, but embodies them metaphorically in the episodic structure of a picaresque tale. In addition to the major linked themes of community, family and individual, careful readers will also note that *I Know Why the Caged Bird Sings* introduces several other themes and images that will characterize Angelou's later writings: the quest for identity and freedom within an environment that has a coherent pattern; the persistence of the past in the present; the necessity of creating one's own world by a transforming act; of seeking, at the price of isolation, one's own truth in the moment of crisis; the drive toward particularity and permanence; the image of the narrator participating vicariously in the heroic act of another. As Angelou develops these themes in *Gather To-*

gether in My Name and in the subsequent volumes of her autobiography, it becomes apparent that they form parts of a larger theme which later writing shows has informed her whole corpus into a theme of transformation (often through transmigration) involving images of death and rebirth. According to one critic, the unsettled life that Angelou records in her autobiography suggests a sense of self as constantly in the process of becoming, of dying and being reborn. Thus, death and rebirth are metaphors that most clearly and comprehensively communicate Angelou's identity.[11] They are the metaphors of psychic and physical growth, from childhood to maturity and womanhood, that Angelou uses to describe the process which the identity-seeker has to go through. Furthermore, the compulsion to repeat the metaphors throughout the autobiography underscores the power of this motif in Angelou's narrative.

A third controlling metaphor of the autobiographical series is embodied in the Easter poem that opens *I Know Why the Caged Bird Sings*:

> What you looking at me for
> I didn't come to stay.
> I just come to tell you that today is
> Easter Day.[12]

These words that she stumbles over during an Easter morning church service at the Colored Methodist Episcopal Church in Stamps, Arkansas, open her narrative with what Angelou takes to be a determinative event in her childhood, and thus convey the pattern of mobility that characterized her formative years.

The form that an autobiography takes is as revealing as its style and content. By placing the poem in a prologue to her narrative, Angelou emphasizes its significance in her life. The poetic statement is not only descriptive of her rootlessness but is also a blues metaphor that foreshadows a cyclical pattern of renewal, rebirth, change in consciousness, and the circuitous journey of recovered innocence. By circuitous journey, I mean the movement of the individual consciousness toward an increasing understanding of the self and where the self stands in relation to the group. The movement toward this goal is an educational process ending in the attainment of self-knowledge as wisdom and power. For Angelou, the journey involves more than her seeking of her identity. As one of the controlling metaphors of the autobiography, the journey or quest is for self-knowledge (which is different from identity), and especially, for resurrection—the triumph of life over death.

Throughout her serial autobiography, Angelou is concerned with narratives that move from misunderstanding to reconciliation. Her quest is, therefore, a universal and timeless one for wholeness and wisdom. Such a quest, one discovers, is indeed the principal matter of Angelou's autobiography, shaping it thematically and structurally and focusing on the spiritual, religious, moral and psychological centers of the individual. Through this quest, Angelou moves away from disorder (misunderstanding or chaos) toward order (reconciliation).

One critic suggests that blues autobiographers[13] depend, from the beginning of their works, upon some particular aspect of their character to act as a lens through which the confusion of experience can be perceived and the integrity of personality achieved.[14] Wright, for example, opens his autobiography (*Black Boy*) with a primal scene from his childhood in which the young Richard, bored and resentful, seeks amusement by burning his mother's long fluffy white curtains, which later ignite the house. Wright uses this scene to dramatize the complex nature of his early struggles with his environment, which was characterized by fear, violence, racial insecurity, and beatings. The process of discovering meaning in the blues autobiography is closely associated with the process of discovering personal consciousness. In her recitation of the Easter poem, Angelou, the child and solitary persona, engages and confronts the audience with an essentially contradictory situation in that it is the young Maya's "shield,"[15] her means of proclaiming isolation, while at the same time, defending against its infringement.

The thematic challenge of the rhetorical questions repeats itself elliptically in the second sentence ("I didn't come to stay" [for you to look at]). The resolution of the situation in the third sentence, being reflective, turns back upon the apparent contradictoriness to resolve it. One might ask, how so? First, the rhetorical question establishes the ironic tone which contrasts sharply with the implicit celebratory promise of the risen Christ. A subtext to the question presumes that there is something to look at, to draw the audience's attention to the speaker. What might that something be? Symbolically, it is the persona as Christ, a reminder of the cyclical renewal. But this, like the content of experience, has meaning for the audience only upon reflection after the last word of the poem. In the meantime, in the last two sentences, the I/Christ reveals that the purpose is to remind "you" that "today" is the day for reflecting upon the Risen One, the One who is, in essence, the Self. The latter twist focuses upon the audience as the ultimate "I" as in traditional blues[16]; and, in turn, individually, the audience becomes the Christ, arisen and renewed. The secular complement to the religious metaphor is, of course, the idea of progress expressed in both the autobiography and poetry. The resurrection imagery is most clearly conveyed in the poetry collection *And Still I Rise*, a title that suggests the resurrection of Christ and reiterates, indirectly, an important theme in the autobiographical series. Indeed, the poetic introduction to *I Know Why the Caged Bird Sings* reinforces the theme of ascension; returning and leaving (motion) form a pattern in Angelou's autobiography, a making of peace with her past so that, in retrospect, it is neither a sentimental haven nor a cage.

What characterizes Angelou's circuitous journey—her movement toward self-knowledge—is mutability, emerging from and strengthened by her repeated movement, reorientation and assimilation, through which Angelou the autobiographer consciously records an evolution of identity that represents a synthesis of the extremes of her paternal grandmother and her mother. While the three women emerge as pragmatists, each is different in relationship to the set of values out of which Angelou operates.

At the heart of Angelou's autobiography, then, is the single traditional focus: the growth of the individual from innocence to knowledge. The tone is exuberant and confident. The autobiography expresses strongly held convictions and is vibrant with a commitment that will allow no room for ambiguity.[17] Autobiography enables Angelou to resurrect and commemorate both ordinary and unique aspects of her childhood, youth, and adulthood, thereby understanding, as clearly as possible, those formative experiences that forge her mature identity. Thus, for Maya Angelou, autobiography is an evocation of the human spirit.

2

Initiation and Self Discovery

... We are a tongued folk. A race of singers. Our lips shape words and rhythms which elevate our spirits and quicken our blood. ... I have spent over fifty years listening to my people."
—Maya Angelou

". . . I think of my life and the lives of everyone who has ever lived, or will ever live, as not just journeys through time but as sacred journeys."
—Frederick Buechner,
The Sacred Journey

"The longest journey is the journey inwards."
—Dag Hammarskjöld, *Markings*

Until Maya Angelou published the first volume of her autobiography, no one could have predicted that she would achieve such popular recognition, as distinct from the esteem which many Black writers had long enjoyed in academic and literary circles, i.e., Sterling Brown, Langston Hughes, Gwendolyn Brooks, Robert Hayden and Margaret Walker. *I Know Why the Caged Bird Sings*, published in 1970, broke ground in terms of critical acclaim, and large sales throughout the country presaged the success soon afterwards of such writers as Rosa Guy, Louise Merriwether, Verta Mae Grosvenor, and Alice Walker.

Maya Angelou started writing relatively late in life and was forty-one when *I Know Why the Caged Bird Sings* was published. Her adult life up to then had been a dizzying succession of mini-careers, many of which are described in the five volumes of the autobiography. For Angelou, however, the autobiographical mode was to become the means to an enduring public career. Written at the urging of friends who were overwhelmed and fascinated by the stories she told about her childhood, her grandmother in Arkansas, and her mother in California, Angelou recalls that she was "roped" into writing this first volume:

> At the time, I was really only concerned with poetry, though I had written a television series. James Baldwin took me to a party at Jules and Judy Feiffer's home. We enjoyed each other immensely and sat up until three or four o'clock in the morning drinking scotch and telling tales. The next morning Judy Feiffer called a friend of hers at Random House and said, "You know the poet Maya Angelou? If you can get her to write a book . . ."
> When Robert Loomis, Judy's friend and an editor at Random House called, I told him that I was not interested. Then I went to California to produce a series for WNET. Loomis called me two or three times, but I continued to say that I was not interested. Then, I am sure, he talked to Baldwin because he used a ploy which I am not proud to say I haven't gained control of yet. He called and said, "Miss Angelou, it's been nice talking to you. But I'm rather glad that you decided not to write an autobiography because to write an autobiography as literature is a most difficult task." I said, "Then I'll do it." Now that's an area I don't have control of yet at this age. The minute someone says I can't, all of my energy goes up and I say, "Yes I can." I believe all things are possible for a human being, and I don't think there is anything in the world I can't do.[1]

On February 12, 1970, the date on which *Caged Bird* was

launched publicly, critics had no reason to think that a first book by an entertainment personality would be of particular importance, although on that day the book received a noteworthy review in *The New York Times*. Shortly thereafter, in the March 2, 1970 edition of *Newsweek*, critic Robert A. Gross praised *Caged Bird*, noting that it

> was more than a tour de force of language or the story of childhood suffering because it quietly and gracefully portrays and pays tribute to the courage, dignity and endurance of the small, rural Southern Black community in which [Angelou] spent most of her early years in the 1930's.[2]

At about the same time, Edmund Fuller observed, in his *Wall Street Journal* review that

> Only the early signs of artistry and intellectual range are in this story, but their fulfillment are as evident in the writing as in the accomplishments of Maya Angelou's varied career.[3]

Before the end of the year, other critics were heralding *Caged Bird* as marking the beginning of a new era in the consciousness of Black men and women and creating a distinctive place in Black autobiographical tradition.

I Know Why the Caged Bird Sings (hereafter called *Caged Bird*) is a carefully conceived record of a young girl's slow and clumsy growth. It is also a record of her initiation into her world and her discovery of her interior identity. In *Caged Bird*, Angelou first confidently reaches back in memory to pull out the painful times: when she and her brother Bailey fail to understand the adult code and, therefore, break laws they know nothing of; when they swing easily from hysterical laughter to desperate loneliness, from a hunger for heroes to the voluntary pleasure-pain game of wondering who their *real* parents are and how long it will be before they come to take them to their *real* home. Growing up in Stamps, Arkansas, as Maya Angelou describes those long-ago years, is a continual struggle against surrender to the very large adults, who, being Black, practiced and taught special traditions whose roots were buried in Africa or had been created during centuries of slavery. According to these traditions, a good child dropped her eyes when speaking to an adult; a good child spoke softly; a good child never resisted the idea that Whites were better, cleaner, or more intelligent than Blacks. Growing up and surviving as a young girl in the South of the 1930s and early 1940s is a painful experience for a young girl whose world is colored by disillusion and despair, aloneness, self-doubt, and a diminished sense of self.

Indeed, Angelou underscores her diminished sense of self and the rootlessness of her early childhood years when she proclaims in the prologue:

> "What are you looking at me for?
> I didn't come to stay . . ."[4]

The words are painfully appropriate, for the young Maya, then Marguerite Johnson, is a shy, tensely self-conscious child who believes that her true beauty is obscured. As she struggles to remember her lines, she is conscious of her dual self, which is the constant subject of her fantasies. Beneath the ugly disguise—a lavender taffeta dress remade from a White woman's discard, broad feet, and gap-teeth— is the real Marguerite.

Such fantasies are ephemeral and the time comes when the young girl must face the painful reality of her being. Angelou recalls that

Easter's early morning sun had shown the dress to be a plain ugly cut-down from a white woman's once-was-purple throwaway. It was old-lady-long too, but it didn't hide my skinny legs, which had been greased with Blue Seal Vaseline and powdered with Arkansas red clay. The age-faded color made my skin look dirty like mud, and everyone in church was looking at my skinny legs.[5]

For Maya there is no magical metamorphosis, no respite from her "black dream." On this Easter Sunday, she understands the futility of her wish to become "one of the sweet little white girls who were everybody's dream of what is right with the world."[6] Unlike Christ, whose resurrection from death the church is commemorating, Maya cannot be reborn into another life where she will be White and perfect and wonderful.[7] Pained by this reality and by the impossibility of her White fantasy, Maya flees from the church "peeing and crying" her way home.

This scene recreates graphically the dynamics of many young Black girls' disillusionment and imprisonment in American society. In *Black Rage*, psychiatrists William H. Grier and Price M. Cobb describe this "imprisonment":

If the society says that to be attractive is to be white, [the Black woman] finds herself unwittingly striving to be something she cannot possibly be; and if femininity is rooted in feeling oneself eminently lovable, then a society which views her as unattractive and repellent has also denied her this fundamental wellspring of femininity.[8]

The young Maya not only lives in a society which defines beauty in White terms of physical beauty, but she also internalizes these notions. In a letter (February 4, 1966) to her long-time friend Rosa Guy, Angelou wrote, "My belief [as a child] that I was ugly was absolute, and nobody tried to disabuse me—not even Momma. Momma's love enfolded me like an umbrella but at no time did she try to dissuade me of my belief that I was an ugly child."[9]

In this letter and in the autobiography as well, Angelou

offers important insights into the effects of social condi-
tioning on the mind and emotions of a Black child growing
up in a hostile environment. Writing from the perspective
of adulthood, the older Angelou reveals that, within this
imprisoning environment, there is no place for the young
Maya; that she is a displaced person whose pain is inten-
sified by her awareness of her displacement.[10]

> If growing up is painful for the Southern Black girl, being aware
> of her displacement is the rust on the razor that threatens the
> throat. It is an unnecessary insult.[11]

Such truths characterize important segments of Angelou's
life and provide wide-ranging, significant themes for the
work.

Yet Angelou does not relate all facets of her childhood
experiences. Rather, through a series of episodic chapters,
she selects and chronicles those incidents from which she,
as a girl-child, learned valuable, life-determining truths
about the world, about her community, and about herself—
truths incarnated in moments of insight (initiation) and discovery of self. By identifying these epiphanies, the reader
is able to define the unique vision of the work and its precise
and individual illumination of reality.

After the prologue, the reader meets two children, ages
three and four, who are wearing wrist tags that identify
them as Marguerite and Bailey Johnson, Jr. A note addressed "To Whom It May Concern" states that they are
traveling alone from Long Beach, California, to Stamps,
Arkansas, to the care of Mrs. Annie Henderson. Angelou
explains that she and her brother Bailey were shipped to
the home of their paternal grandmother when their parents
decided to end their calamitous marriage. The porter, who
was charged with their welfare, ends his assignment the
next day in Arizona, but before leaving the train, he pins

their tickets to Bailey's inside coat pocket. From that day until the day of their arrival in Stamps, the children are literally on their own. This episode further defines the dynamics underlying Angelou's battered self-esteem. Early on, when the young Maya fantasizes that she is White, blond and beautiful, she does so because, in reality, she sees herself as a child whom no one could possibly love, certainly not her mother or father who have so totally rejected her.

Maya and Bailey reach safely their destination and gradually adjust to their new life in Stamps, becoming integral parts of Grandmother Henderson's store and religion, of Uncle Willie's life, and of the community itself, a community that closes around the children "as a real mother embraces a stranger's child. Warmly but not too familiarly."[12]

There are nights when Maya and Bailey cry and share their loneliness as unwanted children who have been abandoned by their divorced parents. They also share their questions: Why did they send us away? What did we do so wrong? Why, at three and four, did we have tags put on our arms to be sent by train alone from Long Beach, California to Stamps, Arkansas, with only the porter to look after us?[13] Unable to accept the fact that they have been abandoned, Maya and Bailey convince themselves that their mother is dead because they cannot bear the thought that she "would laugh and eat oranges in the sunshine without her children."[14] Comforted by the imagined reality of her mother's death, Angelou, recalling the child's emotional response, writes:

I could cry anytime I wanted to by picturing my mother (I didn't know what she looked like) lying in her coffin. Her hair, which was black, was spread out on a tiny little pillow and her body was covered by a sheet. The face was brown, like a big O, and

since I couldn't fill in the features I printed M O T H E R across
the O, and tears would fall down my cheeks like warm milk.[15]

Angelou recalls vividly the assault to the young Maya's
diminished sense of self when she receives her mother's
first Christmas presents. The tea set and a doll with blue
eyes, rosy cheeks and yellow hair are all symbols of a White
world foreign to the child's experience. Not only is her
mother alive, as the presents prove, but Maya, the five-
year old herself, has been, the forgotten child during her
two years of separation from her mother. The young Maya
may, in time, be able to forgive her mother, but for the
moment she must face the unimaginable reality of being
both unwanted and abandoned.

Even if Angelou had focused on only the psychological
trauma of her early years or had merely probed the fragile
relationship between the environment and her coming-of-
age, *Caged Bird* would merit the critical acclaim it has received. Clearly, the autobiography does much more. While
Angelou constantly demonstrates the "unnecessary insult"
of Southern Black girlhood in her passage from childhood
to adolescence, at the same time she skillfully recreates
those psychic, intellectual, and emotional patterns that
identify her individual consciousness and experience. In
doing so, the autobiographer gives concrete embodiment
to such significant themes as Death, Regeneration, and Rebirth, and thus, makes a creative and imaginative use of
the Christian myth.

Angelou's childhood is molded by her wise, hard-work-
ing grandmother, Mrs. Annie Henderson, in a community
where weekly church services, periodic revival meetings,
and occasional confrontations with Whites punctuate the
young girl's education. A tough-minded business woman
who purchased her store and first parcel of land in 1910
with $1,000 in dimes earned from her sale of meat pies and

lemonade, Grandmother Henderson is not demonstrative in her love for Maya. Yet she is uncompromising in that love. A model of righteous behavior and a source of knowledge and pride, she sustains the young Maya during one of the most difficult periods of her life. Moreover, she gives the child the kind of nurturing that will later fortify her to face her growing-up years and the outside world. From a childhood still vivid in her mind, Angelou recalls that "a deep-brooding love hung over everything she touched."[16]

Through this indomitable woman, Maya is introduced to the spiritual side of Black life. Portrayed as an individual whose world is ordered by work, duty, "her place," and religion, Grandmother Henderson represents the religious tradition begun in secret praise meetings during slavery and further developed in the small frame churches that once dotted the countryside and small American towns. Much of the strength of the Black woman in general and of Grandmother Henderson in particular can be attributed to the Black church. From slavery to emancipation, Blacks found solace in the Biblical injunction to "refrain thy voice from weeping, and thine eyes from tears: for thy work shall be rewarded . . ." (Jeremiah 31:16). A strongly devout woman, Grandmother Henderson begins each morning with a traditional prayer of thanks and supplication, one often heard in Black American churches through individual witness and testimony:

> Our Father, thank you for letting me see this New Day. Thank you that you didn't allow the bed I lay on last night to be my cooling board, nor my blanket my winding sheet. Guide my feet this day along the straight and narrow, and help me to put a bridle on my tongue. Bless this house and everybody in it. Thank you, in the name of Your Son, Jesus Christ, Amen.[17]

To Grandmother Henderson, God is a real and personal

friend. In the spirit of many Black Americans of her time, her understanding of Biblical teachings has persuaded her that Blacks are God's chosen vessels, that He will punish those who torment His people. As God protected the Jews from Pharoah, she believes that God, in His own time and in His own way, will protect and deliver Blacks. Until that day comes, she teaches Maya and Bailey to rely on the promises of a just God, to avoid contact with Whites where possible, and to follow the paths of life that she and her generation had found to be safe ones. She also teaches them to respect piety and those customary laws that governed all areas of a "good" child's life and behavior. According to this rigid code, cleanliness is next to Godliness, dirtiness the inventor of misery. An impudent child is not only detested by God and a shame to its parents, but will also bring destruction to its house and life. Through the purity of her life and the quality of her discipline, Mrs. Annie Henderson demonstrates that, by centering one's being in God, one can endure and mitigate the effects of an unjust world. Angelou internalizes these silent lessons. Indeed, she owes much of her clarity of vision to her grandmother, who though not always able to protect herself and family from the exterior climate of hate, refuses to diminish herself as a human being by succumbing to bitterness or by engaging in aggressive, retaliatory behavior. Like any caring adult who has been charged with the responsibility of rearing a child, Mrs. Henderson knows that she must not only interpret society to Maya but also equip her with the pertinent skills and attitudes that will allow her to survive. While she is often unrelenting in her punishment (i.e., when she gives Maya a severe beating for using the expression "by the way") and has little time or inclination to verbalize affection, Mrs. Henderson does manage to usher Maya safely through her childhood and early adolescence.

Angelou recalls that in Stamps "segregation was so complete that most Black children didn't really, absolutely know what Whites looked like."[18] Yet the White world remained an ever-hovering, dreaded threat. Total awareness of this threat led to a clearly defined pattern of behavior on the part of Blacks and respect for certain codes of conduct if one was to survive in the South. One respected, though unwritten, law was "The less [one said] to Whitefolks (or to even powhitetrash) the better. . . ." Moreover, as Angelou writes, Momma "didn't cotton to the idea that Whitefolk could be talked to at all without risking one's life."[19]

Angelou's consciousness of the oppression suffered by Black Americans is honed by the realities of Maya's daily experience, the most difficult of which force her to acknowledge that like Grandmother Henderson, Uncle Willie and Bailey—like all those she knows to be good and worthy—she is also bound to be affected by forces outside her control or comprehension.

Angelou recalls a painfully confusing incident that occurred when she was 10 years old, an incident that she later would judge to be a pivotal experience in her initiation because it taught her an important lesson about her grandmother's ability to survive and triumph in a hostile environment. The incident involves three young White girls who are known to nettle Blacks and who have come onto Grandmother Henderson's property to taunt the older Black woman with their rudeness, to ape her posture and mannerisms, and to address her insolently by her first name. Throughout this scene, she stands solidly on her porch, smiling and humming a hymn. When their actions produce no results, the girls turn to other means of mockery, making faces at Mrs. Henderson, whispering obscenities, and doing handstands. The young Maya, who observes this painful scene from inside the store and suffers humiliation for her grandmother, wants to confront the girls directly, but she realizes that she is "as clearly imprisoned behind the scene as the actors outside [are] confined to their roles."[20]

Throughout the incident, Mrs. Henderson is a pillar of strength and dignity, standing tall and firm. As the girls take leave, they yell out in succession, "Bye, Annie." Never turning her head to acknowledge their departure or unfolding her arms, she responds, "Bye, Miz Helen, 'bye Miz Ruth, 'bye Miz Eloise."[21] Enraged by her grandmother's seeming subservience and powerlessness, Maya cries bitterly. Later, however, when she looks up into the face of her grandmother, who is quietly standing over her, she sees her face as "a brown moon that [shines] on [her]." Angelou recalls this moment:

> She was beautiful. Something had happened out there, which I couldn't completely understand, but I could see that she was happy. Then she bent down and touched me as mothers of the church lay hands on the sick and afflicted—and I quieted.
>
> "Go wash you face, Sister." And she went behind the candy counter and hummed, "Glory, glory, hallelujah, when I lay my burden down."
>
> I threw well water on my face and used the weekday handkerchief to blow my nose. Whatever the contest had been out front, I knew Momma had won.[22]

This scene is a dramatic, symbolic recreation of the kind of spiritual death and regeneration Angelou experienced during the shaping of her development. But it is also a vivid recapturing of Black/White tensions in the South of the 1930s. On the one hand, three White girls, attempting to use their race as an overbearing instrument of power, treat a Black woman like another child, practicing the rituals of

White power with the full sanction of the White community and attempting to reduce the Black woman to their level. On the other hand, the Black woman chooses the dignified course of silent endurance. Although Mrs. Henderson knows that she must accord the girls some modicum of respect, she refuses to recognize them as anything but White children, refuses to register their offensiveness or humanity, refuses to play their game. Seeking to preserve her own integrity and to transcend the ugliness of their actions, Mrs. Henderson wins a psychological victory by using this weapon to transcend the limitations of her social world.[23]

White dominance intrudes on other occasions that also teach Maya vital lessons in courage and survival and open her eyes to the fact that she belongs to an oppressed class. In Uncle Willie, for example, she sees the dual peril of being Black and crippled when he is forced to hide in the potato bin when the sheriff casually warns Grandmother Henderson that local White lynchers will be on a rampage in the Black community. Through this terrifying experience, Maya learns that lameness offers no protection from the wrath of bigots.

Other occasions provide proof of a predatory White world and of White ritualistic violence against the Black male, for example, when Bailey sees the castrated body of a Black man. Horrified by what he has seen but not understood, Bailey begins to ask questions that are dangerous for a young Black boy in the Arkansas of 1940. The incident leads Angelou to conclude bitterly that "the Black woman in the South who raises sons, grandsons and nephews had her heartstrings tied to a hanging noose."[24] Years later, when Angelou must fight for the opportunity to become the first Black person hired as a conductor on the San Francisco streetcar, she learns that White racism is not merely a problem of the South but an evil that penetrates most aspects of American life.

While intrusion from the outside world provides experiences that increase the child's awareness of her social displacement, the Store, where Blacks congregate before and after work, teaches Maya the meaning of economic discrimination. By keenly observing the cotton workers who visit the Store, she gains insight into their inner lives. In the early dawn hours, Maya observes the cotton workers, gay and full of morning vigor, as they wait for the wagons to come and take them to the fields. Optimistic that the harvest will be good and not choosing to recall the disappointments of the recent past, the workers josh each other and flaunt their readiness to pick two or three hundred pounds of cotton this day. Even the children promise "to bring home fo' bits."[25] The later afternoons, however, reveal the actual harshness of Black Southern life. In the receding sunlight, "the people [drag themselves], rather than their empty sacks."[26] Angelou writes:

> Brought back to the Store, the pickers would step out of the backs of trucks and fold down, dirt-disappointed, to the ground. No matter how much they had picked, it wasn't enough. Their wages wouldn't even get them out of debt to my grandmother, not to mention the staggering bill that waited on them at the white commissary downtown.

> The sound of the new morning had been replaced with grumbling about cheating houses, skimpy cotton and dusty rows. In later years I was to confront the stereotyped picture of gay song-singing cotton pickers with such inordinate rage that I was told even by fellow Blacks that my paranoia was embarrassing. But I had seen the fingers cut by the mean little cotton bolls, and I had witnessed the backs and shoulders and arms and legs resisting any further demand.[27]

In cotton-picking time, the late afternoons reveal the harshness of Black Southern life, which in the early morning had been softened by nature's blessing of grogginess, forgetfulness, and the soft lamplight.

While *Caged Bird* vividly portrays the negative social and economic texture of Stamps, Arkansas, Maya Angelou, like many other Black autobiographers, describes the Southern Black community as one that nurtures its members and helps them to survive in such an antagonistic environment. There are numerous examples that demonstrate the communal character of life in Stamps. People help each other. During the Depression when no one has money, Grandmother Henderson employs a system of barter to help her neighbors and thus to save her store. When the wife of an old friend dies and the widower is unable to accept his loss, Grandmother Henderson and Uncle Willie, without a moment's hesitation, invite him to share their home, although space is limited and the guest will have to sleep on a pallet in Uncle Willie's small bedroom. When Bailey does not return from a movie at his usual time, the Black men and women share Grandmother Henderson's concern. One member's concern becomes the community's concern because members, in their practice of the rituals of extended family relationships, are not only related through the community but through the church as well.

Innumerable passages in *Caged Bird* provide a sense of the Black community, a sense of oneness, a sense of fused strength. The changing seasons, for example, provide opportunities for fellowship and festivity. In winter, after the first frost, hog killings are spirited events that demonstrate community linkages and strength. Everyone is an important participant in this annual rite. As Angelou describes it,

The missionary ladies of the Christian Methodist Episcopal

Church helped Momma prepare the pork for sausage. They squeezed their fat arms elbow deep in the ground meat, mixed it with gray nose-opening sage, pepper and salt, and made tasty little samples for all obedient children who brought wood for the slick black stove. Then men chopped off the larger pieces of meat and laid them in the smoke-house to begin the curing process. They opened the knuckle of the hams with their deadly-looking knives, took out a certain round harmless bone ("it could make the meat go bad") and rubbed salt, coarse brown salt that looked like fine gravel, into the flesh and the blood popped to the surface.[28]

In a very direct way, the church-related activity also speaks to the particularly American value of self-reliance, a value that is necessary for survival in a hostile social world. Unlike the White American, in order for the individual Black American to be self-reliant, he or she must rely on the community.[29]

Angelou's generalized description of a summer picnic fish fry conveys the vigorous solidarity of the entire Black community. Everyone is there: church groups, social groups (Elks, Eastern Stars, Masons, Knights of Columbus, Daughters of Pythias), teachers, farmers, field-workers. Free from their daily chores, excited children run about in wild play and "the sounds of tag beat through the trees."[30]

Musicians perform, displaying their artistry with "cigar-box guitars, harmonicas, juice harps, combs wrapped in tissue papers, and even bathtub basses."[31] The harmony of a gospel group "float[s] over the music of the country singers and melt[s] into the songs of small children's ring games."[32] The amount and variety of food further underscore the importance of the event. The autobiographer recalls:

Pans of fried chicken, covered with dishtowels, sat under benches next to a mountain of potato salad crammed with hard-boiled eggs. . . . Homemade pickles and chow-chow, and baked country hams, aromatic with cloves and pineapples, vied for prominence. . . . On the barbecue pit, chickens and spareribs sputtered. . . . Orange sponge cakes and dark brown mounds dripping Hershey's chocolate stood layer to layer with ice-white coconuts and light brown caramels. Pound cakes sagged with their buttery weight. . . . And busy women in starched aprons salted and rolled . . . fish in corn meal, then dropped them in Dutch ovens trembling with boiling fat.[33]

Through such lyrical reminiscences of childhod, Angelou celebrates the richness and warmth of Southern Black life, and the bonds of community, with all of its possibilities for love and laughter, that often persist in the face of poverty and oppression. In Maya Angelou's vision, both with respect to the Black community and to herself, what is kept consistently in focus is the attempt to preserve and celebrate humanity in the face of seemingly impossible odds. *Caged Bird* testifies to the amazing resilience of Black Americans and their ability to cope with the inequities of American racism. The first volume of her autobiography bears witness to the sense of relationships in the Black community—the cooperative alliances that enable Blacks to survive, with grace and exuberance, the most difficult circumstances. For the young Maya, the Black Community is the essential community.

When Maya is seven years old, she sees her parents for the first time in her memory. Bailey, Sr., making an unexpected visit to Stamps, stuns the child by the reality of his presence. For the first time in her young life, she need create no elaborate fantasies about her father. Bailey, Sr., who has been described by others as a man who had respect for neither morals nor money,[34] is an arrogant show-off, taller than anyone Maya has ever seen and with "the air of a man who [does] not believe what he [hears] or what he himself is [saying]."[35] Yet Maya is fascinated by his ironic pretentiousness. In her fantasy world, her father lives richly, among orange groves and servants, in the kind of elegantly furnished mansions she has seen in the movies. In time, however, Maya learns that he is merely a doorman at the Breakers Hotel in Santa Monica, California. She also learns that her father's real purpose in coming to Stamps is to deliver her and Bailey to their mother in St. Louis. Maya is terrified by the thought of seeing her elusive mother. She wants to beg her grandmother to allow her to remain in Stamps, even if she must promise to do Bailey's chores and her own as well, but she does not have the nerve to try life without Bailey, who is overjoyed by the prospect of joining his "mother dear." The day finally arrives when Maya, bidding a tearful farewell to Grandmother Henderson and Uncle Willie, must leave Stamps behind. A few days after the uneventful trip to St. Louis, Bailey, Sr. returns to California. Maya is neither glad nor sorry when this stranger leaves.

If Bailey, Sr. represents some distant world unknown to Maya, Vivian Baxter's world is equally foreign. Vivian Baxter, Maya's lively, beautiful mother, is bold, self-reliant, and unconventional. Although a trained surgical nurse, she does not work at her profession because neither the operating room nor the rigid eight-to-five schedule provides the excitement she craves. Rather, she cares for herself and children through liaisons with a variety of live-in "boyfriends" who furnish the necessities and through the extra money she earns cutting poker games in gambling parlors. Men are permitted to remain with Vivian Baxter only as long as they follow her stricts code of conduct; one has been cut and another shot for failing to show proper respect for her prerogatives.

For Maya, Stamps and St. Louis stand in sharp contrast.

In Stamps, there are Grandmother Henderson and the
Store; there are also religious devotion and the acceptance
of one's worldly and racial lot. In the closely knit rural
community, Maya knows all the Black people in town, and
they know her. For the young Maya, Stamps is a symbol
of order; in fact, the orderliness of the store—the carefully
arranged shelves, the counters, and the cutting boards—
reflects the orderliness of her life in general. In St. Louis,
however, Angelou is thrown into her mother's world of
taverns, pool halls, gambling, fast living and fast loving.
This is a far looser environment than Maya had ever known
and one that is devoid of the customary laws that Grandmother Henderson had taught her to respect. The range of
sanctioned behavior is also broader, individuals are less
stringently controlled by moral laws or social pressures,
and relations among individuals are less stable. Although
Maya lives comfortably in St. Louis and is excited by many
aspects of urban life, she remains a stranger among
strangers, mainly because the urban community treats the
individual as individual rather than as part of a group, and
so is powerless to provide her the emotional security she
needs.[36] Moreover, having spent four years in the solitude
of Stamps, Maya is dislocated by the strangeness of her
new environment: the tremendous noise of the city, its
"scurrying sounds,"[37] its frightening claustrophobia.
Grandmother Baxter's German accent and elegant manners
are also unfamiliar. Her mother, aunts and uncles are
equally unreal. St. Louis provides Maya neither sense of
place nor permanence. Indeed, after only a few weeks
there, she understands that it is not her real home:

> In my mind I only stayed in St. Louis a few weeks. As quickly
> as I understood that I had not reached my home, I sneaked away
> to Robin Hood's forest and the caves of Alley Oop where all

reality was unreal and even that changed every day. I carried that same shield that I had used in Stamps: "I didn't come to stay."[38]

Shifted from one temporary home to another, Maya develops a tough flexibility that is not only her protective "shield," but also her means of dealing with an uncertain world. Angelou's evocation of the palpable strangeness of the city derives from her ability, as an artist, to maintain the childlike angle of vision in recreating this phase of her childhood.

Yet, for one brief moment, the child, deluded into a false security, fantasizes that she is at home, at last, with her real father. For that moment, Mr. Freeman, Vivian Baxter's boyfriend and someone whom Maya has come to love and trust, holds her close to him. Mr. Freeman's conscious violation of the child's trust, coupled by the child's own need for attention and physical closeness, leads to a further violation that the eight-year old Maya is too young to understand:

He held me so softly that I wished he wouldn't ever let me go. I felt at home. From the way he was holding me I knew he'd never let me go or let anything bad ever happen to me. This was probably my real father and we had found each other at last. But then he rolled leaving me in a wet place, and stood up.[39]

In the past, Maya's world had included Bailey, Grandmother Henderson, Uncle Willie, reading books, and the Store. Now, for the first time, it includes physical contact; and, while not understanding what has taken place in her mother's bed, she is anxious to repeat the experience which has made her feel so loved and secure.

Many growing young girls, denied the emotional satisfaction of loving, concerned parents, look for emotional support at school or at play; and if they are lucky, they find something that moderates their emotional discontent. Maya, however, finds little compensation of this sort. Her autobiography is singularly devoid of references to rewarding peer asociations during her eight-month stay in St. Louis. She is not only dislocated by her new environment, but is also alienated from any supporting peer relationships.

The second time Mr. Freeman embraces the eight-year old girl, he rapes her. The rape, an excruciatingly painful act which involves Maya in ambiguous complicity, produces confusion, shame, and guilt. The courtroom where Mr. Freeman's trial for rape is held would be imposing to a mature, self-confident adult, but it is shattering to the child whose confusion, shame and guilt are further compounded by the voyeuristic aspects of the open courtroom testimony. When Maya is unable to remember what Mr. Freeman was wearing when he raped her, the lawyer suggests that she, not the defendant, is to blame for her victimization. Bewildered and frightened, Maya denies that Mr. Freeman ever touched her before the rape—partly because, in her confusion, she is convinced of her own complicity in the two sexual episodes but more because of her life-long desire for her mother's love and approval:

> I couldn't say yes and tell them how he had loved me once for a few minutes and how he had held me close before he thought I had peed in my bed. My uncles would kill me and Grandmother Baxter would stop speaking, as she did when she was angry. And all these people in the court would stone me as they had stoned the harlot in the bible. And Mother, who thought I was such a good girl, would be disappointed. . . .

> . . . I looked at [Mr. Freeman's] heavy face trying to look as if he would have liked me to say No. I said no.

> . . . The lie lumped in my throat and I couldn't get air . . . Our lawyer brought me off the stand to my mother's arms. The fact

that I had arrived at my desired destination by lies made it less
appealing to me.[40]

Later, when Mr. Freeman is found murdered, Maya is convinced that he is dead because she lied; that evil flows
through her mouth, waiting to destroy any person she might
talk to. To protect others, she convinces herself that she
must stop talking: "Just my breath, carrying my words out,
might poison people and they'd curl up and die like the
Black fat slugs that only pretended."[41] Acting on this con-
viction, Maya becomes a voluntary mute, Mr. Freeman's
death having provoked not only Maya's spiritual death but
also her quasi-isolation from her world.

In Stamps, Maya could count on the unwavering support
of Grandmother Henderson and the Black community.
However, there is a surprising inability on the part of Vivian
Baxter and her family to provide adequate emotional support for Maya or to understand the psychological difficulties
of an eight-year-old who has been traumatized by rape.
When Maya does not behave as the person they know and
accept her to be, she is punished for being so arrogant that
she will not speak to her family. On other occasions, she
is thrashed by any relative who feels offended by her silence. When the family can no longer tolerate Maya's "grim
presence," Vivian Baxter again banishes Maya and Bailey
to Stamps, Arkansas, fulfilling Maya's prophesy that she
had not come to St. Louis to stay.

Maya welcomes her return to Stamps, where she finds
comfort in the barrenness and solitude of a place where
nothing happens. Of this Angelou writes:

> After St. Louis, with its noise and activity, its trucks and buses,
> and loud family gatherings, I welcomed the obscure lanes and
> lonely bungalows set back deep in dirt yards.
>
> The resignation of its inhabitants encouraged me to relax. They

showed me a contentment based on the belief that nothing more was coming to them, although a great deal more was due. Their decision to be satisfied with life's inequities was a lesson for me. Entering Stamps, I had the feeling that I was stepping over the border lines of the maps and would fall, without fear, right off the end of the world. . . .

Into this cocoon I crept.[42]

In this passage and, indeed, throughout her recaptured childhood years in Stamps, Angelou examines herself introspectively. Though, Angelou, the autobiographer, locates herself in the physical environment of her childhood—in a series of physical scenes—her inward retrospective musings and the interiority that she manages to capture so well are more significant to the reader's understanding of the autobiographer's private self than of the external phenomena from which the musings emerge.

Maya lives in "perfect personal silence"[43] for nearly five years until she meets Mrs. Bertha Flowers, Stamps' Black intellectual, who will become for the adult Angelou her "measure of what a human being can be."[44] Mrs. Flowers throws Maya her "first life line"[45] by accepting her as an individual, not in relation to another person. Moreover, Mrs. Flowers ministers to Maya's growing hunger and quest for individuality by giving her books of poetry, talking to her philosophically about books, and encouraging her to recite poems. Committing poems to memory, pondering them, recalling them when lonely, give Maya a sense of power within herself, a transcendence over her immediate environment.

Maya's "lessons in living" with Mrs. Flowers awaken her conscience, sharpen her perspective of her environment and of the relationship between Blacks and the larger society, and teach her something about the beauty and power of language. Emotionally and intellectually strengthened by this friendship, Maya begins to compose poetic verses and ring songs, and to keep a scrapbook journal in which she records her reactions to and impressions of people, places and events, and new ideas that she is introduced to by books. When she is not yet nine years old, she records her impressions of early pioneer life in Arkansas:

> Such jolting, rumbling, squeaking and creaking! Such ringing of cowbells as the cattle plodded along! and dust—dust—so thick that your mouth was full of grit, your eyes were—oh, very dirty, and your hair was powdered with the reddish Arkansas dust. The sun was hot and the sweat was streaming down your face, streaking through the grime. But you were happy for you were on a great adventure. You and your father and mother, brothers and sisters, and many of your neighbors were moving from your old home in the East. You were going to settle on some rich land in Arkansas. And you were going there not on a train of railroad cars—for there were none—but in a train of covered wagons pulled by strong oxen.[46]

In this passage from Angelou's record of the historical self, one finds excellent documentation of the autobiographer's early facility with language and narrative form.

As Angelou chronicles her movements from innocence to awareness, from childhood to adolescence, there are certain social barriers that she must confront and overcome in order to maintain a sense of self and relative freedom.

For example, Angelou's first confrontation with a White person catapults her into a clearer awareness of social reality and into a growing consciousness of self-worth. This confrontation proves to be a major turning point in her life. During a brief time when she was eleven years old, Maya worked in the home of Mrs. Viola Cullinan, a wealthy, transplanted Virginian. With the arrogance of a Southern White woman whom neither custom nor tradition had taught to respect a Black person, Mrs. Cullinan insults

Maya by calling her Mary rather than Marguerite, a name that Mrs. Cullinan considered too cumbersome. Mrs. Cullinan's attempt to change Maya's name for her own convenience echoes the larger tradition of American racism that attempts to prescribe the nature and limitations of a Black person's identity. In refusing to address Maya by her proper name, the symbol of her individuality and uniqueness, Mrs. Cullinan refuses to acknowledge her humanity. A sensitive, reflective nature, combined with an alert intelligence, enables Maya to comprehend the nature of this insult. She writes:

> Every person I knew had a hellish horror of being "called out of his name." It was a dangerous practice to call a Negro anything that could be loosely constructed as insulting because of the centuries of their having been called niggers, jigs, dinges, blackbirds, crows, boots, and spooks.[47]

Maya strikes back, deliberately breaking several pieces of Mrs. Cullinan's heirloom china. In doing so, she affirms her individuality and value. Through this encounter, the young Maya learns that until the individual is willing to take a decisive step toward self-definition, refusing to compromise with insults, he or she remains in a cage. In short, the individual must resist society's effort to limit his or her aspirations. Only after Maya determines to risk Mrs. Cullinan's outrage and to defy the expectations of others is she able to begin to loose herself, psychologically, from the dehumanizing atmosphere of her environment.

Many American autobiographies besides *Caged Bird*, including *The Narrative of the Life of Frederick Douglass*, *Black Boy*, Maxine Hong Kingston's *Woman Warrior*, *The Autobiography of Malcolm X*, *Black Elk Speaks*, Anne Moody's *Coming of Age in Mississippi*, and others, are structured around a narrative enactment of change on two levels: the personal and psychological on one hand, and the sociohistorical and intellectual on the other. Paradoxically, while Angelou is growing in confident awareness of her strength as an individual, she is also becoming increasingly more perceptive about her identity as a member of an oppressed racial group in Stamps. In Stamps, as throughout the South, religion, sports and education functioned in ways that encouraged the discriminated class to accept the status quo. But Angelou demonstrates how Blacks in Stamps subverted those institutions and used them to withstand the cruelty of the American experience.[48]

In a graphic description of a revival meeting, Angelou recalls her first observation of the relation between Blacks and religion. To the casual observer, the revivalists seem to "[bask] in the righteousness of the poor and the exclusiveness of the downtrodden"[49] and to believe that "it was better to be meek and lowly, spat upon and abused for this little time"[50] on earth. Although the poor give thanks to the Lord for a life filled with the most meager essentials and a maximum amount of brute oppression, the church rituals create for them a temporary transcendence and an articulation of spirit. However, in this tightly written, emotionally charged scene, Angelou briefly records the joining point between the blues and religious tradition. Miss Grace, the good-time woman, is also conducting rituals of transcendence through her barrelhouse blues. The agony in religion and the blues is the connecting point:

> A stranger to the music could not have made a distinction between the songs sung a few minutes before [in church] and those being danced to in the gay house by the railroad tracks. All asked the same questions. How long, oh God? How long?[51]

Early on, the reader gleans that although the Joe Louis victories in the boxing ring in the 1930s were occasions for

street celebrations that caused tens of thousands of Blacks
to parade, sing, dance, and derive all the joy possible from
these collective victories of the race, for Angelou, Joe
Louis' victory over heavy-weight contender Primo Carnera
was "a grotesque counterpoint to the normal way of life"[52]
in Arkansas. Angelou describes the scene that takes place
in her grandmother's store on that night of the fight, vividly
recapturing John Dunthey's style and language:

Louis is penetrating every block. . . . Louis sends a left to the
body and it's the uppercut to the chin and the contender is drop-
ping. He's on the canvas, ladies and gentlemen."

Babies slid to the floor as women stood up and men leaned toward
the radio.

"Here's the referee. He's counting, One, two, three, four, five,
six, seven . . . Is the contender trying to get up again?"

All the men in the store shouted, "No."

"—eight, nine, ten." There were a few sounds from the audience,
but they seemed to be holding themselves in against tremendous
pressure.

"The fight is all over, ladies and gentlemen. Let's get the micro-
phone over to the referee . . . Here he is. He's got the Brown
Bomber's hand, he's holding it up . . . Here he is . . ."

Then the voice, husky and familiar, came to wash over us—"The
winnah, and still heavyweight champeen of the world . . . Joe
Louis."

Champion of the world. A Black Boy. Some Black mother's son.
He was the strongest man in the world. People drank coca-colas
like ambrosia and ate candy bars like Christmas. Some of the men
went behind the Store and poured white lightning in their soft-
drink bottles, and a few of the bigger boys followed them. Those
who were not chased away came back blowing their breath in
front of themselves like proud smokers.

It would take an hour or more before the people would leave the

Store and head for home. Those who lived too far had made arrangements to stay in town. It wouldn't do for a Black man and his family to be caught on a lonely country road on a night when Joe Louis has proved that we were the strongest people in the world.[53]

Angelou even remembers her graduation from elementary school not as the customarily exciting and happy occasion for the young graduates and their families and friends, but as a dramatization of the painful injustices of a segregated society and an underscoring of the powerlessness of Blacks within that society. As she listens to the insulting words of an oblivious and insensitive White speaker, the young girl perceives a terrifying truth about her racial self and about the desperation of impotence, especially about the impotence of. Black people in the South of the 1930s:

It was awful to be Negro and have no control over my life. It was brutal to be young and already trained to sit quietly and listen to charges brought against my color with no chance of defense. We should all be dead.[54]

Yet, her momentarily mixed feelings of despair, shame and anger on her graduation day at the seemingly hopeless future for young Blacks in racist America are surmounted by her pride in Blacks when the Negro National Anthem is sung. As Maya consciously joins the class and audience in singing, she unconsciously, from her perspective in time, also predicts her own future as a poet:[55]

We survived. The depths had been icy and dark, but now a bright sun spoke to our souls. I was no longer simply a member of the proud graduating class of 1940; I was a proud member of the wonder, beautiful Negro race.

Oh, Black known and unknown poets, how often have your auctioned pains sustained us? Who will compute the only night made less lonely by your songs, or by the empty pots made less tragic by your tales?

If we were a people much given to revealing secrets, we might raise monuments and sacrifice to the memories of our poets, but slavery cured us of that weakness. It may be enough, however, to have it said that we survive in exact relationship to the dedication of our poets (include preachers, musicians and blues singers).[56]

But after Grandmother Henderson and Maya are insultingly ejected from the office of a White dentist and told that he would rather stick his hand "in a dog's mouth than in a nigger's,"[57] the child can only compensate for such painful impotence by fantasizing power and triumphant revenge.

Angelou's complex awareness of what Black men, women and children encountered in their struggles for selfhood is apparent in each of these incidents. Such experiences are recorded not simply as historical events, but as symbolic revelations of Angelou's inner world. They are social, geographic and psychological occasions. The implication that one's powerlessness in the larger world may need to be experienced and overcome in the process of personal development is very clear.

In 1941, when Maya is thirteen, she and Bailey move to Oakland and later San Francisco to live with their mother whom they have not seen in six years. By this time, Vivian Baxter has married Daddy Clidell, a gambler and respected businessman, who will soon become "the first father [Maya] would know."[58] For a while, Maya re-experiences some of the personal dislocation already felt so acutely in Stamps and St. Louis. But in time "the air of collective displacement [and] the impermanence of life in wartime"[59] dissipate her sense of not belonging. Of this she writes:

In San Francisco, for the first time I perceived myself as part of
something. . . . The city became for me the idea of what I wanted
to be as a grownup. Friendly but never gushing, cool but not frigid
or distant, distinguished without the awful stiffness.[60]

In San Francisco, the tender-hearted girl changes into
another imagined self: a compound of her mother, Mrs.
Flowers, and Miss Kirwin of Washington High School.

Just as Stamps and St. Louis stood in sharp contrast, so
do San Francisco and Stamps. From her prosperous stepfather, Maya receives a basic ghetto education:

He owned apartment buildings and, later, pool halls, and was
famous for being the rarity "a man of honor." He didn't suffer,
as many "honest men" do, from the detestable righteousness that
diminishes their virtue. He knew cards and men's hearts. So during the age when Mother was exposing us to certain facts of life,
like personal hygiene, proper posture, table manners, good res-
taurants and tipping practice, Daddy Clidell taught me to play
poker, blackjack, tonk and high, low, Jick, Jack and the Game.
He wore expensively tailored suits and a large yellow diamond
stickpin. Except for the jewelry, he was a conservative dresser
and carried himself with the conscious pomp of a man of secure
means.[61]

In San Francisco, Maya is also introduced to a colorful
cast of urban street characters (i.e., Stonewall Jimmy, Just
Black, Cool Clyde, Tight Coat and Red Leg) who make
their living through gambling and trickery. Here she learns
a new morality: the Black American ghetto ethic by which
"that man who is offered only the crumbs from his country's table . . . by ingenuity and courage, is able to take of
himself a Lucullan feast."[62] Mr. Leg's story, for example,
is an excellent portrayal of such an individual and a brilliant
recapturing of the trickster motif found in African and Afro-
American literature. Through trickery, Mr. Red Leg, a con

artist and a hero-figure of Black American urban folklore, outwits his White antagonist. In doing so, he symbolizes the strength, dignity, and courage Black Americans are able to manifest in spite of their circumscribed lives, although they might function as miscreants, not only in the eyes of the White world but also to the preachers and matriarchs within the Black community. Black men like Mr. Red Leg, who use "their intelligence to pry open the door of rejection and [who] not only [become] wealthy but [get] some revenge in the bargain,"[63] are heroes to Maya and her "Black associates."[64]

Three other experiences further dramatize Angelou's awareness of self and her world, changing with sometimes bewildering speed, and help her to work out new patterns of selfhood and personal direction.

When she accompanies "Daddy Bailey" on a vacation to Mexico, he, having drunk quantities of tequila at a roadside bar where he has taken Maya, goes off with "his woman," leaving Maya with strangers and no money. Hours later, he returns, too drunk to drive. Rather than spending the night in the car in Mexico, Maya, who has never driven a car, manages to drive down the circuitous mountain road some fifty miles, to cross the border, and to return them safely to California. Angelou recalls:

> The challenge was exhilarating. It was me, Marguerite, against the elemental opposition. As I twisted the steering wheel and forced the accelerator to the floor, I was controlling Mexico, and might and aloneness and inexperienced youth and Bailey Johnson, Sr., and death and insecurity, and even gravity.[65]

Unlike any of her former experiences in Stamps, this single experience proves to Maya that she can indeed have power over her life and destiny.

Soon after their return to California, there is a bitter argument between Maya and Dolores (her father's current "girlfriend"), who wants Bailey's daughter out of her home and her life. Urging Maya to return to her mother, Dolores calls Vivian Baxter a whore. When Maya slaps her, Dolores cuts Maya severely. After taking her to one friend for emergency medical care, Bailey, Sr., leaves her with a second friend. Knowing that violence would ensue if she returned home and her mother learned that she had been cut, Maya leaves without telling her father or his friend, and after wandering about San Diego for some while, joins a junkyard commune of homeless children whom she describes as "the silt of war frenzy."[66] After she has spent a month in the commune, Maya's thought processes have altered so significantly that she is hardly able to recognize her former self. Her peers' unquestioning acceptance dislodges her familiar feelings of insecurity; moreover, the unrestrained life that she experiences within the group expands her spiritual horizons and "initiates [her] into the brotherhood of man."[67] The gratitude Angelou owes those who befriended her on her passage from childhood to adolescence to adulthood will forever include her junkyard family:

> After hunting down unbroken bottles and selling them with a white girl from Missouri, a Mexican girl from Los Angeles and a Black girl from Oklahoma, I was never again to sense myself so solidly out of the pale of the human race. The lack of criticism evidenced by our ad hoc community influenced me, and set a tone of tolerance for my life.[68]

Time and time again, Angelou brings us to the question of human relationships. Through the junkyard experience, she learns that, beyond the barriers of race, all men and women are the same; they share the same fears, the same loneliness, and the same hopes. The commune experience also confirms Angelou's determination to exercise further control over her being and helps her to establish a valuable new direction for her personal growth. Months later when Angelou becomes the first Black hired as a conductor on the San Francisco streetcars, her determination and success in this venture can be directly attributed to these pivotal experiences in Mexico and California.

Angelou must confront and overcome one other obstacle before she can begin to know herself. This problem relates to numerous questions about her sexuality that plague her when she is convinced, after her third reading of *The Well of Loneliness*, that she is verging on lesbianism: Why are her voice so heavy and her hands and feet so far from being feminine and dainty? Why are her breasts so sadly underdeveloped? Is she a lesbian? Do lesbians bud gradually "or burst into being with a suddenness that dismayed them as much as it repelled society?"[69] For weeks, Angelou seeks answers to these questions, probing into unsatisfying books and into her own unstocked mind without finding a morsel of peace or understanding. When she finally approaches her mother to seek answers to the questions about her sexuality and about the disturbing physical changes that are taking place in her body, Vivian Baxter gently reassures her daughter that the physical changes are just human nature. Not altogether convinced by her mother's assurances, Maya decides that she needs a boyfriend to clarify her position to the world and to herself. From her point of view, "a boyfriend's acceptance of [her] would guide [her] into the strange and exotic lands of frills and femininity"[70] and at the same time, conrirm her heterosexuality. But among her associates, Maya cannot find an interested partner. Taking matters into her own hands, she decides to offer herself to a neighborhood youth; and, at sixteen, she becomes pregnant, a surprise consequence of a single, impersonal, unsatisfactory experiment.

Like the "aloneness" that she has experienced most of her life, Maya is literally "alone" during most of her pregnancy, for she manages to keep this fact hidden from her mother, her teachers, and her friends for eight months and one week. When Vivian Baxter learns from Maya that she will deliver a child shortly, she nurtures her daughter with understanding and support and, in doing so, becomes the compassionate, loving mother of Maya's childhood fantasies. The birth of Maya's son is a celebration of a new life, of Maya's own rebirth as a young mother, and of Maya's discovery of her creative self. But it is also an ironic outcome of a completely loveless and casual relationship.

The final scene of *Caged Bird* is richly symbolic. Maya is reluctant to let her three-week old baby sleep with her because she is certain that she will roll over in the night and crush him. But Vivian Baxter ignores her daughter's fears and places the baby beside his mother. The next morning, Vivian Baxter is standing over her daughter. Under the tent of blanket which Maya has devised with her elbow and forearm, the baby sleeps soundly. Vivian Baxter whispers to her daughter, "See, you don't have to think about the right thing. If you are for the right thing, then you do it without thinking."[71] This scene verbalizes Vivian Baxter's faith in Maya's instinctive qualities of motherhood and Maya's acceptance of herself as a creative, life-giving force.

By the end of *Caged Bird*, the displaced young Maya has found a place and has discovered a vital dimension of herself. No longer need she ask, "What you looking at me for?", or fantasize a reality other than her own. By the end of the autobiography, Angelou, the young adult, has succeeded in freeing herself from her cage by assuming control of her life and fully accepting her womanhood. Indeed, as Sidonie Smith posits, with the birth of her child, Angelou is herself born into a mature engagement with the forces of life. In welcoming that struggle, Angelou refuses to live a death of quiet submission:[72]

> Few, if any, survive their teens. Most surrender to the vague but murderous pressure of adult conformity. It becomes easier to die and avoid conflicts than to maintain a constant battle with the superior forces of maturity.[73]

Roy Pascal observes that autobiography acquires its shape through the autobiographer's consciousness of what the child ultimately became. Angelou is able to confront her memories of her own past with honesty, humor and irony because they form a necessary part of her spiritual and intellectual development. She believes, as most autobiographers do, that memory affords access to the past that is worth revealing and that an understanding of the human condition—not information about a life, but insight into its process—is intrinsically valuable.

The narrative voice at work in *Caged Bird* is that of the older autobiographer who is not only aware of the journey, but also enlarged by it, an achievement that is emphasized by the affirming nature of the work. In *Caged Bird*, Maya Angelou undergoes the archetypal American journey of initiation and discovery.

3

The Contradictory and Imaginative Selves

". . . Whatever the pain, I do not deny the past."
—The *San Francisco Chronicle*
May 22, 1974

I have been given an adventurous spirit and the ability to forgive myself. The Biblical title of my second autobiographical volume symbolizes my belief that many women and men, although they may never admit it, have had similar experiences. Until such time as they too have the need to tell the truth until it hurts, these men and women can gather together in my name and be heard.
—The *Chicago Tribune*
May 30, 1974

In writing *Gather Together in My Name*, I had to scrape off all the awards and honors to deal with those experiences—to admit them all. It was more difficult to write about these experiences in 1973 than it would have been ten years earlier. Yet, if by my revelations I can encourage anybody first to avoid some of the things I experienced; and if they haven't avoided them, if I can encourage them to forgive themselves, it's all worth it.
—*San Jose Mercury News*
June 2, 1974

In *Caged Bird*, Maya Angelou focused on themes that are typical of American literature in general and of Black American literature in particular: the individual quest for self-discovery and the personal search for a meaningful identity and self-sustaining dignity in a difficult social environment. Through the development of these themes, Angelou illuminated Black survival by dramatizing how Black men, women and children transcend racial obstacles. While Stamps, St. Louis, Oakland, San Francisco, and Mexico represented the geographical boundaries of her quest, the destination was no longer a place but a state of mind because Angelou had sought and achieved an increased intellectual and emotional awareness of herself and her world. Thus, by the end of *Caged Bird*, the quest had become also an interior journey, suggestive of one critic's theory that autobiography presupposes the autobiographer's intention to reflect his or her inward realm of experience.[1] It is this "inward realm of experience" that Angelou managed to capture so well in *Caged Bird* and that she explores and reveals more intimately in *Gather Together in My Name*. As Angelou continues to examine the question, "What kind of self am I?", this volume comes to represent both a new stage in her self-knowledge and a new formulation of responsibility towards the self.

Most autobiographers succeed better with their childhood than with their later life, even their youth. This success, it has been suggested, might be ascribed partly to the strength of an established literary tradition; for, however different children and their circumstances may be, their mode of apprehension and growth is much more similar than in later life. Nonetheless, in *Gather Together in My Name*, as in *Caged Bird*, Maya Angelou wields firm control over her readers as she chronicles a series of first experiences that a maturing Maya undergoes in her effort to find her own moral center and to develop a completeness of being: first love, her first experience with marijuana, her first experience as a cook, her discovery of Russian writers, her humiliating experiences as both a scapegoat and the object of her former classmates' derisiveness, her first encounter with Vivian Baxter's violence and legendary rage, her initiation into show business, her first internalization of her role as mother, her short-lived careers as Madam, prostitute, and fencer.

While there is obvious stylistic and thematic uniformity in *Caged Bird* and *Gather Together in My Name* (hereafter referred to as *Gather Together*), the latter is a somewhat shorter, less multi-layered work. Two reasons may account for this difference. Perhaps the primary reason is the design that Angelou consciously imposed on this volume of the autobiography, coupled with her own self-imposed censoring of details. Commenting on the design of *Gather Together*, Angelou has observed:

> There is a fragmentary climate in childhood which makes it generally impossible to believe in one's future and simultaneously to disbelieve in one's mortality. I tried, sometimes unsuccessfully, to capture the episodic, erratic nature of adolescence in *Gather*.[2]

This episodic quality of the story becomes, therefore, a faithful reflection of the autobiographer's fragmented, disjunctive adolescence.

The second reason relates to Angelou's artistic maturity at this stage of her writing career. In *Caged Bird*, which provided a training exercise for *Gather Together* and her subsequent works, Angelou structured the autobiography around selected pivotal events in her childhood that led to significant epiphanic experiences. In addition, she probed those events, both introspectively and retrospectively, so as to identify important thematic clues about the relationship between her childhood experiences and her developing self. However, by the time that she began to write *Gather Together*, four years after the publication of her first volume of poetry (*Just Give Me a Cool Drink of Water 'fore I Diiie*), Angelou was in the process of learning the art of condensation. As a result, in *Gather Together*, her style has both matured and simplified. That is to say, her style is more telegraphic and condensed, a quality which enables her to transmit emotion and understanding in sharp and vivid word images that provide keys to the deeper meaning of the work as well as to the unconscious motivations of the autobiograpaher. For example, in describing her introduction to Russian novelists, Angelou writes:

> During this time when my life hinged melodramatically on intrigue and deceit, I discovered the Russian writers. . . . Life, as far as I had deduced it, was a series of opposites: black/white, up/down, life/death, rich/poor, love/hate, happy/sad, and no mitigating areas in between. It followed Crime/Punishment.

> The heavy opulence of Dostoevsky's world was where I had lived forever. The gloomy, lightless interiors, the complex ratiocinations of the characters, and their burdensome humors, were as familiar to me as loneliness.

> I walked the sunny California streets shrouded in Russian mists. I fell in love with Karamazov brothers and longed to drink from a samovar with the lecherous old father. Then Gorki became my favorite. He was the blackest, most dear, most despairing. The books couldn't last long enough for me. I wished the writers all alive, turning out manuscripts for my addiction. I took to the Chekov plays and Turgenev, but always returned in the late nights, after I had collected my boodle, to Maxim Gorki and his murky, unjust world.[3]

At other points in the narrative, she writes:

> The South I returned to . . . was flesh-real and swollen-belly poor.[4]
> . . .

I clenched my reason and forced their faces into focus.[5]

. . .

Their conversations were tightly choreographed measures, and since I didn't know the steps, I sat on the sidelines and watched.[6]

. . .

At home, life stumbled on.[7]

Even in these short passages, taken out of context, one senses the palpability, the precision, and the rhythm of Angelou's writing.

The violation which began in *Caged Bird* takes on a much sharper focus in *Gather Together*. Here, Angelou searches for stability and security, a search which takes both outward and inward forms. Outwardly, she searches for such securities as a good-paying job, a comfortable home for herself and son, a dependable family relationship. But inwardly, she seeks to anchor her fluctuating inner life by finding a steady relationship (love) and establishing a sense of unity in her life. The emotion of love and the sentiment of loyalty, which help so much to order and focus one's psychic life, are curiously absent in *Gather Together*. Because of her loveless existence, Angelou experiences, therefore, a loneliness that becomes, at times, suicidal and contributes to her unanchored self.

Moreover, the constant shifts in locale enforce a sense of fragmentation and chaos. Unlike *Caged Bird*, in which the young Maya developed in two primary physical locations and within a relatively closed group of people, in *Gather Together*, a maturing Maya constantly meets new people and either discards them or is abandoned by old ones. The instability of human relationships and the resulting loneliness are pointedly underscored in the repeated dissolution of Angelou's relationships. Throughout the autobiography, the cycle continues and little sense of stability or a constant social environment arises.

What distinguishes *Gather Together* is the harmony it evokes between the autobiographer's outward experience and her inward growth, between incidents in the life of Maya Angelou and her spiritual digesting of them, so that each experience becomes a part of a process and a revelation of something within the personality of the maturing young woman. The life that Angelou reveals in *Gather Together* is presented, therefore, as a life in process. Uncertain of who she is or what she will become, the adolescent Maya tries out various roles to determine which one is most authentic. This restless, frustrated, trying-on of roles is an instructive process of self-education in which Angelou undergoes a variety of experiences that will continue her passage from innocence towards maturity and adulthood.

A courageous work, *Gather Together* is one of the most personally revealing autobiographies written by an American of Angelou's stature. Except for Wright's *Black Boy*, and perhaps Claude Brown's *Manchild in the Promised Land*, it is difficult to cite another American autobiography in which the writer bares so openly his or her shortcomings and those of other Blacks. Although, as with most autobiography, Angelou has been selective in recounting this period of her life, it is to her credit that she does not seem to allow any consideration to supersede her responsibility to reveal all that she can possibly discover concerning her life or concerning the difficulties that she personally confronted in achieving selfhood. In *Gather Together*, an artistically more mature work than *Caged Bird*, Angelou transcends the boundaries of adolescence to embrace more universal concerns about independence, self-reliance, and self-fulfillment.

The fragmented texture of the larger American society at the end of World War II serves as an appropriate backdrop for the reader's introduction to the alienated and fragmented nature of Angelou's life. In the Prologue to *Gather Together*, Angelou describes, in graphic language, the confusion and disillusionment that struck the Black community when all the economic progress achieved during World War II evaporated in peacetime air. The War, Angelou observes, had afforded Blacks their first opportunity to demonstrate their large-scale ability to perform as factory workers and as government and military personnel at all levels of skill. Further, the war crisis had provided them with a unique opportunity to demonstrate, for all to see, the difference between the American creed and practice. The democratic ideology and rhetoric with which the war was fought stimulated a sense of hope and certainty in Black Americans that the old race structure was destroyed forever, for "Hadn't [Blacks and Whites] all joined together to kick the hell out of *der Gruber*, and that fat Italian, and put that little rice-eating Tojo in his place?"[8] Large numbers of Blacks believed that, with the end of World War II, race prejudice would be dead, and that their sacrifices, which had won the nation victory, would be repaid in full measure.

Following World War II, however, the expected White acquiescence in a new racial order did not occur. Even though the sacrifices of Blacks had helped to win the victory, they were offered no assurances that "the good times were coming":[9]

Two months after V-Day, war plants began to shut down, to cut back, to lay off employees. Some workers were offered tickets back to their Southern homes. Back to the mules they had left. . . . No good. Their expanded understanding could never again be accordioned within these narrow confines. . . .

. . . Military heroes of a few months earlier, who were discharged from the army . . . began to be seen hanging on the ghetto corners like forgotten laundry left on a backyard fence. Their once starched khaki uniforms were gradually bastardized. An ETO

jacket, plus medals, minus stripes, was worn with out-of-fashion
Zoot pants. The trim army pants . . . were topped by loud, color-
crazed Hawaiian shirts. . . . Only the shoes remained. The Army
had made those shoes to last. And dammit, they did.[10]

Yet Angelou suggests that, throughout American history,
Black Americans have been among the most avid seekers
of the American dream, believing that if they could but
grasp the dream, they could walk in dignity. So fervid had
been the Black American's pursuit of the dream that in
every war, including World War II, Black leaders had offered up young Black men and women, the strength of the
race, as proof of their worth as Americans. Notwithstand-
ing, in the aftermath of World War II, the dream again
proved elusive. Angelou emphasizes this fact in her graphic
reconstruction of the economic fabric of the Bay Area Black
community in 1945 and in her description of the texture of
the people's lives.

The end of the war is for Angelou a time of disillusionment and self-doubt in the real world outside childhood.
This new odyssey focuses on the autobiographer's passage
from adolescence to young adulthood between the ages of
seventeen and nineteen and involves settings in San Francisco, Los Angeles, Stamps, and in various other parts of
California. During this uneasy period in her life, Angelou
must find support for herself and her infant son while pur-
suing her own personal independence and direction. As she
struggles desperately to fulfill her destiny as mother and
woman, she must also continue her struggle to establish an
appropriate niche within her family and to secure her fragile
relationship with her mother. This relationship, which she
explored in *Caged Bird*, is a part of the continuing insecurity that she portrays in *Gather Together*. A more subtle,
less obvious reason for this insecurity relates to the young
mother's strong feelings of guilt about her illegitimate son,

feelings that the adult Angelou never fully explores or explicates in her autobiography. Early on, however, it is clear that the teenage Angelou is haunted by these feelings of guilt because she is a product of a rural, southern upbringing, and that she has retained the sense of religion and morality instilled in her by her grandmother. At one point, she writes: "My son had no father—so what did that make me? According to the Book, bastards were not to be allowed into the congregation of the righteous."[11] Angelou is alone in her struggle to come to terms with her dilemma, for neither her mother nor Bailey can assist her search for emotional security nor help her to resolve her recurring financial problems.

To support herself and her son, Angelou becomes a Creole cook and shake dancer in San Francisco, a cocktail waitress in Los Angeles, and an absentee madam of a two-woman house of prostitution near Bakersfield. Nonetheless, she maintains a perspective that separates the sordid from her own self-appraisal and dreams of a better future. For the most part, the men she meets are destructive to themselves and their women. For example, she has a brief affair with an older man who introduces a new warmth and excitement into her life and tempts her into a prostration of gratitude but who leaves her abruptly and without explanation. She falls in love with a show business partner who abandons her for an older, drug-shattered former love. And in her continuing quest for love and security, she is inveigled into a short-lived career of prostitution by a forty-five-year-old pimp and briefly assumes the role of heroine-prostitute, struggling to get her man out of financial difficulty. Angelou's tough, honest telling of the tale is richly enhanced by retrospective self-knowledge:

I had managed in a few tense years to become a snob on all levels, racial, cultural, intellectual. I was a madam and thought myself morally superior to the whores. I was a waitress and believed myself cleverer than the customers I served. I was a lonely unmarried mother and held myself to be freer than the married women I met.[12]

Although readers have had by now an overexposure in American literature to the world of prostitution and pimps, con men and street women, and drug addiction and spiritual disintegration, Maya Angelou provides, almost, a new view of these negatives through her sharp portrayal of the fragmented lives that urban life in America sometimes fosters. In doing so, she reveals a more selective vision of Black American life. Under the pressures of a loveless existence, Angelou witnesses the decline of her brother into drug addiction and is herself saved from the cul-de-sac of drugs by the kindness of an addict friend who exposes her to the nauseous act of administering heroin to himself in order to repel her from the temptation. Recognizing her own innocence, Angelou writes, "My escapades were the fumblings of youth and to be forgiven as such."[13] But even as she forgives herself for her youthful fumblings, a maturing Angelou insists on taking full responsibility for her life and for that of her child.

Throughout the autobiography are variations of the theme of death and rebirth; and, the interplay between the individual and the group, the outsider and the tradition, the streetfolk and the collective Black experience.

Adolescence, like childhood, is full of contradictions. As with Angelou, however, these contradictions are often diverse expressions of a common theme, the search for oneself and one's place in the world. While much of what the adolescent Angelou does may, on first reading, strike one as somewhat bizarre, a closer examination of the work reveals that, beneath the superficial posturing and poses, runs a thread of idealism through much of her behavior. In fact, as in *Caged Bird*, the young Maya yearns for something beyond the reality which she tries again and again to transform. In *Gather Together*, the adolescent Maya is busy losing old illusions and building new ones to take their place. At times, she is convinced of the hopelessness of all illusions, old and new, and lapses into cynicism and despair, no less genuine for the melodramatic display she makes of them. Furthermore, her idealism is often at war with her own private yearnings, making her painfully aware of her contradictory and imaginative self, hungering for the ultimates of existence, sometimes coming to terms with reality. In *Gather Together*, Angelou's ridiculous posturing and contradictory behavior, and the feigned independence of an adolescent girl in the throes of growing up, are superimposed for one's own life. Uneducated and therefore available for only the most menial jobs, Angelou is carried through terrifying situations of the human spirit which involve constant assaults on her self-esteem.

A main strand of Black autobiography, one critic suggests, takes the reader on a journey through chaos, a pattern established by the narratives of escaped slaves. This journey, which is both psychic and physical in form and which encompasses a primary theme in Black autobiographical tradition, derives from an erosion of faith in the American dream idea which earlier had provided grounds for optimism.[14]

Maya, the child-woman, begins her "journey through chaos" when, at the age of seventeen and in a mixture of arrogance and insecurity, she refuses the offer of her mother and stepfather to leave her infant son in their care in order that she can return to school and prepare for her future. Angelou recalls:

I refused. First I reasoned with the righteous seriousness of youth,

I was not Daddy Clidell Jackson's blood daughter and my child was his grandchild only as long as the union between Daddy and Mother held fast. . . . Second, I considered that although I was Mother's child, she had left me with others until I was thirteen and why should she feel more responsibility for my child than she had felt for her own.[15]

Insecurity, coupled with self-doubt, leads Angelou to quit her mother's home and to get a job and a room of her own so that she can prove to the whole world that she "was equal to [her] pretensions."[16] The loss of the security of Vivian Baxter's home provides the beginning point of Angelou's psychic journey and further enhances her loss of self-worth. Angelou's quest for a new home becomes, therefore, tantamount to her parallel quest for feelings of self-worth.

Maya Angelou's psychic journey, which accentuates the assault on her self-esteem, intensifies when she fails a simple intelligence test and is denied employment as a telephone operator but is offered a job as a bus girl in the telephone company's cafeteria. Although she accepts the job, she hates it so much that she quits after one week because she cannot endure the offense of cleaning up after the White trainee operators who had been her high-school classmates. Continuing, the journey subsequently includes the numerous dismal jobs that Angelou must accept; the men who move in and out of her life; the strange love affairs in which she is inevitably the victim; and, in an effort to overcome her deep despair and isolation, her brief flight to Los Angeles in the hope that her aunts and uncles, who are childless, will take her and her young son to their bosoms. Too late, however, she realizes that they are "not equipped to understand that an eighteen-year-old mother is also an eighteen-year-old girl."[17] A close-knit group of fighters, these aunts and uncles have no patience with weakness and only contempt for losers. In their world, "people . . . paddled their own canoes, pulled their own weight, put their own shoulders to their own plows and pushed like hell."[18] When she is rejected by her mother's family, Angelou is forced to play the Baxter game of independence and to pretend that she has merely been passing through Los Angeles en route to San Diego to visit her father.

Despair deepens even more when Angelou applies for enlistment in the WACs and is first accepted but then rejected when she fails the loyalty test because it is learned that, between the ages of fourteen and fifteen, she studied dance and drama at the California Labor School, now proscribed as a Communist organization. As is evident in her unsuccessful attempt to join the army, full of naive, ironic patriotism and economic hope, nothing is more painfully clear in *Gather Together* than the fact that Angelou, like most Black Americans of the time, was very much dedicated to the American dream of success. Yet, it must be noted that, at this point in her development, the adolescent Maya is very much a product of the Hollywood upbringing and of her own romanticism when she writes:

> On the silver screen they would have vied for me. The winner would have set me up in a cute little cottage with frangipani and roses growing in the front yard. I would always wear pretty aprons and my son would play in the Little League. My husband would come home . . . and smoke his pipe in the den as I made cookies for the Boy Scouts meeting.
>
> I was hurt because none of this would come true. . . .[19]

Throughout *Gather Together*, Angelou's creation of imagined realities is central to the structural pattern and meaning of the work.

The most resonant incident in the autobiographer's psychic journey occurs when Angelou undertakes a physical journey to Stamps, Arkansas, fleeing to the emotional security of her childhood home. The return to Stamps by train, setting memories in motion, balances the early desire of the autobiographer to move beyond her immediate home into the larger world. As Angelou moves past the sights, sounds, and smells of the town, memories come back:

> In my memory, Stamps is a place of light, shadow, sounds and entrancing odors. The earth smell was pungent, spiced with the odor of cattle manure, the yellowish acid of the ponds and rivers, the deep pots of greens and beans cooking for hours with smoked or cured pork. Flowers added their heavy aroma. And above all, the atmosphere was pressed down with the smell of old fears, and hates, and guilt.

> On this hot and moist landscape, passions changed with the ferocity of armored knights colliding. . . . I took its being for granted and now, five years later, I was returning. . . .[20]

For Angelou, then, there is a sense of timelessness in the "cage" of her youth, not because she sees the place and its inhabitants as human archetypes, but because something of Stamps has remained a part of her. In Stamps, there are no great surprises for Angelou; the new sensations are the old ones, and the traveler on the hot southern road is the voyager within. Returning and leaving form, therefore, a pattern in *Gather Together*—the pattern of a circuitous journey, a making of peace with the past so that, in retrospect, Stamps seems neither a sentimental haven nor a cage.

Angelou's stay in Stamps ends painfully when she is ordered out of town by her beloved Grandmother Henderson. Before Maya leaves, however, Grandmother Henderson administers a violent, protective reprimand to her granddaughter, whose behavior has been sharpened by big-city ways, because she has endangered the safety of the family and community by responding to a White shopkeeper's abuse of her by engaging in some unacceptable abuse of her own. In this scene, the reader is reminded that the Black community of Angelou's childhood and youth discouraged individuality out of self-defense. Since Grandmother Henderson had learned through harsh experience that the whole group could be punished for the actions of a single member, her violent reprimand was an efficient form of behavior control and training, even for a young woman who was destined to return to San Francisco. Recalling that forced return to California, Angelou explains:

> Momma's intent to protect me had caused her to hit me in the face, a thing she had never done, and to send me away to where she thought I'd be safe. So again, the South and I had parted and again I was headed for the cool gray hills of San Francisco. I raged on the train that white stupidity could dictate my movements and I looked unsheathed daggers at every white face I saw.[21]

After this brief and discomforting visit, Angelou returns to California to cook in a greasy, dingy, diner, knowing that the rancid cooking oil and the old men's sadness had seeped into her pores. A few months of tap-dancing provide only a brief interlude in her life, for she reaches an all-time low and finds herself drawn towards heroin. Teetering on the brink of destruction, Angelou is given a sudden glimpse into the hidden world of the wretched, a world into which she is poised to fall.

However, in a paradoxical way, her story of drifting disillusionment ends, somewhat abruptly, and becomes a celebration of life, when a drug addict ("slouched, nodding, his mouth open and . . . saliva sliding down his chin as slowly as the blood had flowed down his arm")[22] exposes himself to teach Maya a lesson. The end of *Gather Together* achieves the honed understatement of a deeply felt truth:

The life of the underworld was truly a rat race, and most of its inhabitants scurried like rodents in the sewers and gutters of the world. I had walked the precipice and seen it all, and at the critical moment one man's generosity pushed me away from the edge.[23]

The generosity of Troubadour Martin, Maya's drug addict friend, gives Maya that rebirth into innocence. Thus, in this passage the older Angelou retrieves knowledge only dimly perceived by the nineteen-year-old protagonist.

Roy Pascal argues that beyond factual truth, beyond the "likeness," an autobiography has to give that unique truth of life as it is seen only from the inside. The autobiographer must, therefore, design a mode for structuring the narrative and for presenting truth.[24] For example, the autobiographer may organize his or her life around a central symbol or image to suggest that all crucial experiences are relevant to one central aspect of the writer's being, as Maya Angelou does in *Caged Bird*. Or the autobiographer may employ various stances to define his or her character and to serve as the organizing principle of the work. In *Gather Together*, Angelou employs such devices as humor and self-mockery, portraiture of the contradictory and imaginative selves, and fantasy. For the most part, Angelou is successful in her utilization of these devices, but, at other times, she is less so. For example, humor and self-mockery become, at times, a substitute for a deeper look, a closer examination of behavior, motivation, attitude. However, because Angelou refuses to gloss over her stupidities and mistakes or to ignore her ridiculous posturing or feigned sophistication, humor and self-mockery become, in part, Angelou's means of achieving distance in her work. To her credit, Angelou has the power of joking at herself, of recreating the past in a humorous spirit without demeaning other people involved, and of capturing the pathetic and painful overtones of experiences through laughter in order not to be overwhelmed by them.

Note Angelou's bittersweet memory of her train trip from San Francisco to Los Angeles to visit the Baxters:

Being from The City, I had dressed for the trip. A black crepe number which pulled and pleated, tucked and shirred, in a wrap all its own. It was expensive by my standards, and dressy enough for a wedding reception. My short white gloves had lost their early-morning crispness during the ten-hour coach trip, and Guy, whose immensity matched his energy, had mashed and creased and bungled the dress into a very new symmetry. . . . In spite of the wrinkled dress and in spite of the cosmetic case full to reeking with dirty diapers, I left the train with my son a picture of controlled dignity. I had over two hundred dollars rolled in scratchy ten-dollar bills in my brassiere, another seventy in my purse, and two bags of seriously selected clothes. Los Angeles was going to know I was there.[25]

Note also Angelou's humorous yet bittersweet recollections of her dance audition in San Francisco for R. L. Poole, who later becomes her dance partner, and of her fateful excursion into downtown Stamps to purchase a dress pattern. An older Angelou humorously recaptures her dance audition.

As my legs slipped apart and down, I lifted my arms in the graceful ballet position number one and watched the impresario's face race from mild interest to incredulous. My hem caught mid-thigh and I felt my equilibrium teeter. With a quick slight of hand I jerked up my skirt and continued my downward glide. I hummed a little snatch of song during the last part of the slither, and kept my mind on Sonja Henie in her cute little tutus. Unfortunately, I hadn't practice the split in months, so my pelvic bones resisted with force. I was only two inches from the floor, and I gave a couple of little bounces. I accomplished more than I planned. My skirt seams gave before my bones surrendered. Then my left foot caught between the legs of Mother's heavy oak table, and the other foot jumped at the gas heater and captured the pipe that ran from the jets into the wall. Pinned down at my extremities with the tendons in my legs screaming for ease, I felt as if I were being crucified to the floor, but in true "show must go on" fashion I kept my back straight and my arms uplifted in a position that would have made Pavlova proud. Then I looked at R.L. to see what impression I was making. Pity at the predicament was drawing him from his chair. . . . My independence and privacy would not allow me to accept help. I lowered my arms and balanced my hands on the floor and jerked my right foot. It held on to the pipe, so I jerked again. I must have been in excellent shape. The pipe came away from the stove, as gas hissed out steadily like ten fat men resting on a summer's day. . . . There was no doubt that R.L. Poole had just witnessed his strangest audition.[26]

Of her three-mile walk into downtown Stamps she writes:

I dressed San Francisco style for the nearly three-mile walk and proceeded through the black part of town, past the Christian Methodist Episcopal and African Methodist Episcopal churches and the proud little houses that sat above their rose bushes in grassless front yards, on toward the pond and the railroad tracks which separated white town from black town. My postwar Vinylite high heels, which were see-through plastic, crunched two inches into the resisting gravel, and I tugged my gloves all the way up to my wrist. I had won over the near-tropical inertia, and the sprightly walk, made a bit jerky by the small grabbing stone, the neat attire and the high headed position, was bound to teach the black women watching behind lace curtains how they should approach a day's downtown shopping. I would prove to the idle white women, once I reached their territory, that I knew how things should be done. And if I knew, well, didn't that mean that there were legions of Black women in other parts of the world who knew also? Up went the Black status. When I glided and pulled into White Town, there was a vacuum. The air had died and fallen down heavily. . . . Then I realized that the white women were missing my halting but definitely elegant advance on their town. I then admitted my weariness, but urged my head higher and my shoulders squarer than before.[27]

Yet this refusal to let herself off easily and the self-mockery which is her means to honesty sometimes become a masking of a central truth. For example, the adult Angelou provides a similarly humorous recollection of her adolescent self when she describes, at the end of Chapter 6, her adoration of her one-time lover Curly, a description which provides humor rather than insight.

> I was so happy that the next day I went to the jewelers and bought him an onyx ring with a diamond chip. I charged it to my stepfather's account.[28]

Instead of reflecting on this act retrospectively and from the distance of adulthood, as she has viewed other experiences in *Gather Together*, the older Angelou simply ridicules herself, a response which is not a substitute for reflective commentary. Angelou's is an ironic, mocking humor, and her jokes and humor are finely tuned. Yet nothing is merely humorous in *Gather Together*. And at no point does Angelou use humor merely to detract readers from her true feelings. Behind the laughter, behind the comic spirit is the adult's vision of human frailty.

In *Gather Together*, Maya Angelou presents a moving portrait of the contradictory adolescent self, and, at times, the autobiography is a comedy of self-deception. However, the various acts and thoughts of the protagonist are never presented as odd twists and turns within a complex character. They are consistently the unresolved contradictions of an adolescent's being. One senses this during Angelou's moments of self-pity and guilt about her son's illegitimacy when the adolescent Maya is quite willing to play the role of the wronged young girl who has been left pregnant by "a low-down bastard"[29] and to conveniently obliterate from her mind the memory that she had initiated the sexual tryst with her son's father. Further, when Curly leaves her, she pretends to be strong and independent but enjoys her role as the jilted heroine, "deserted yet carrying on."[30] At the height of her illicit prostitution business, she joins a Baptist church and stands in the choir singing the old songs with great feeling. And while she enjoys the large bank account that she has accrued from her business, she wants "the money without name, the ease without strain."[31] During the two-and-a-half months when Angelou plays the role of Madam, she operates at the points of a stylistic triangle: in front of the lesbian prostitutes she is braggadocio; at the cocktail lounge where she has her legitimate job, she is the picture of modest servitude; and with Mother Cleo, the landlady/babysitter who reminds her of Grandmother Henderson, she is the innocent young mother. Maya's power of contradiction is boundless. Even in Stamps, especially when Grandmother Henderson is not around, she stands with hand on hip and head cocked to one side, speaking of the wonders of the West and the joy of being free, while conveniently forgetting that she has fled to Stamps for "protection," that if life were so grand in San Francisco she would not have returned to the dusty mote of Arkansas. And although she wants to experiment with hard drugs, she does not wish to be exposed to the ugly realities of the drug world.

A revelation of youthful foolishness usually implies that something will take its place, that something within the character's being will build slowly to edge it out. This is not always the case in *Gather Together*. Angelou's innocence must re-establish itself at the beginning of each episode in order for her behavior to highlight the contradictory nature of her adolescent self. Nonetheless, one of the strengths of *Gather Together* is that at no point is the adolescent Maya wise before the event. She matures as she chronicles these years of her life and her gaining of wisdom is an often painful, tragi-comic experience.

In *Gather Together*, Angelou's imagination interacts with and transforms her environment. In doing so, it often creates the reality that saves her. When, for example, she is hurt by the coolness of the Baxters' reception in Los Angeles, she becomes the star of her own melodrama and fantasizes:

> . . . one day I would be included in the family legend. Some day, as they sat around in the close circle recounting the fights and feuds, the pride and prejudices of the Baxters, my name would be among the most illustrious.[32]

In Stamps, the confrontation with the store clerk stems from Maya's insistence on playing a role. Uppity Maya, sharpened by big-city ways, fantasizes that she is indeed an elegant, sophisticated San Francisco lady. Thus, for a few moments, the dusty General Merchandise Store *is* San Francisco's Emporium, and Maya *is* an arrogant San Francisco matron reprimanding a silly, insensate clerk. As she begins to smoke marijuana more and more, she develops new postures and fantasizes about new dreams, many of which result from what she has seen in movies. She longs for a job as a companion/chauffeurette to a boss who is the image of Lionel Barrymore. Somewhat later, even though the Poole-Rita dance partnership creates in her a longing for the stage and for the bravado of an audience, she dreams of finding a permanent love and marriage. Because of her strong desire for the June Allyson screen-role life, she agrees to become the older L.D.'s "Bobby Sock Baby" and a prostitute as well, in hopes of attaining a life of ease and romance. The foolish Maya even fantasizes about becoming the wife of her generous drug-addict friend Troubadour Martin and using heroin to prove her loyalty to him in order to gain a permanent relationship and security. The entire work emphasizes the role of fantasy as a creative force in Angelou's growth. Throughout the autobiography, the narrator's imagination yearns for something beyond her reality. Thus, she uses the imagination not only to savour and stretch experience, but also to make her reality bearable.

Throughout the narrative, Maya is brave, tenacious, and hopeful in a way which transcends the unrealistic optimism of many contemporary autobiographies. It is primarily Angelou's imagination that helps her to keep her identity intact while teaching her to act out roles of survival. Finally, what Angelou explores in *Gather Together* is the state of the relation between the romantic imagination—innocence—and the objective reality to which it ultimately must be reconciled.

In *Gather Together*, Angelou acknowledges defeat and vividly recreates the alienation and fragmentation that characterized her life. She does so not because she wishes to reinforce a sense of defeat or victimization but to ensure that we all learn to recognize what constitutes vulnerabilty in order that we can avoid the consequences. This recognition forces one to acknowledge the sources of one's pain and to reconcile oneself to bearing, in some degree, responsibility for that pain.[33]

Entering squalid humiliation and returning from it whole and hopeful, *Gather Together in My Name* binds pain and humor together through its unique voice. While Angelou knows some of life's pleasures, she also knows its pain and offers up her autobiography as an extraordinary testament of disappointment and celebration.

4

The Adult Self in Bloom

Until I married at twenty-one, I had a Hollywood induced illusion that a husband . . . would come along and take the burden of my life from my shoulders. I dreamed that this fictional person would make every decision for me, from the most profound to the most frivolous. After I was married, I found that rather than being grateful to the decision maker, I resented intrusions into the privacy of my will. I have discovered that one probably learns more from one's mistakes than from one's triumphs, and I reserve the right as a human being to make my own mistakes.

—Maya Angelou

What quickens my pulse now is the stretch ahead rather than the one behind, and it is mainly for some clue to where I am going that I search through where I have been, for some hint as to who I am becoming or failing to become that I delve into what used to be. I listen back to a time when nothing was much farther from my thoughts than God for an echo of the gutturals and sibilants and vowellessness by which I believe that even then God was addressing me out of my life as he addresses us all. And it is because I believe that, that I think of my life and the lives of everyone who has ever lived or will ever live, as not just journeys through time but as sacred journeys.

—Frederick Buechner
The Sacred Journey

Apart from the genuine pleasure that childhood recollections can evoke, or the relief one feels in looking back at a closed chapter of adolescent turmoil, having survived life's vicissitudes and having developed sound foundations for growth mean that one can carry into adulthood those qualities of freshness, enthusiasm, and emotional involvement that stand an individual in good stead throughout life. When an individual can live with his or her past without being bogged down by it, the individual remains adaptable, but, more importantly, capable of continued growth.[1]

Maya Angelou demonstrates the truth of this assertion in the third and fourth volumes of her autobiography, *Singin' and Swingin' and Gettin' Merry Like Christmas* and *The Heart of a Woman*. Here, she moves into the adult world, and into the White world and the international community as well, confirming the belief that all of an individual's experiences fuse into his or her personality. Here also, Angelou continues to write honestly about her romantic dreams and fantasies, her pretensions and ambition, her connections with her past, her vulnerability, and her growth and survival. In doing so, she provides not only an extended definition of the self, but also a graphic portrait of the adult self in bloom.

Singin' and Swingin' and Gettin' Merry Like Christmas is a much different book from *Caged Bird* and *Gather Together*. It is different because the experiences on which it is based are much different from those which inspired the earlier books. In them, Angelou called forth from memory a period marked by disappointments and humiliations and by psychic growth. However, the third volume marks years of joy in Angelou's life and the title tells the story in *Singin' and Swingin' and Gettin' Merry Like Christmas* (hereafter referred to as *Singin' and Swingin'*). Borrowed from Black folklore, the title is symbolic of the beginnings of Angelou's success and fulfillment as an entertainer, singing and dancing in California clubs, and as an adult. *Singin' and Swingin'* takes the reader on a sunny tour of Angelou's twenties and plots the genesis of a performer. Marguerite Annie Johnson of Stamps, Arkansas, and Rite, Sugar, and Rita—pseudonyms for prior personae—fall away as she comfortably inhabits her new name, Maya Angelou. As one reads this work, one discovers that it is a continuing story, one told in the existential present.

While the above is an accurate summation of the third volume, it would greatly misrepresent the work to imply that it contains only joy. During the years 1949 through 1955, the period covered by *Singin' and Swingin'*, Angelou continues to be plagued by a central problem: the tough texture of poverty that forces her to hold on to a series of unrewarding jobs in order to support herself and her son. But like the cunning heroine in a picaresque novel, this self-conceived picaresque heroine has learned to live by her wits, to survive, and at times, to prosper.

Singin' and Swingin' opens with a scene of personal displacement in which Angelou's loneliness and aloneness, coupled with her separation from family and community, are sharply delineated. Under these new circumstances, Angelou examines her attitudes and her relationship with the larger community—the White community—as she comes in intimate contact with Whites for the first time. In Stamps, Blacks and Whites lived separately and opportunities for shared positive experiences did not exist. Also, in California, Angelou's experiences were confined largely to the Black community. But before Angelou is free enough to enter into any positive relationship in the larger community, she must examine and discard her stereotypical views about Whites, although she is aware that many of these views have been used by Blacks as a survival strategy to shield their Black vulnerability. The maturity that Angelou gains in this section of the autobiography from a hard examination of her views and feelings and from her racial encounters will be later manifested in her more tolerant acceptance of other races. However, before she can achieve this maturity, Angelou must live through new experiences that will test her in new ways.

The first test comes when Angelou is unexpectedly given a job in a record shop by the White female co-owner. Unaccustomed to kindness from Whites, she is confused by this overture of friendship. Yet she needs the job. And, although certain that the proprietor has ulterior motives and hidden prejudices, Angelou accepts the work. To her surprise and relief, she gradually discovers that her fears are groundless. This incident frames the course of the first section of *Singin' and Swingin'*. Conditioned by earlier experiences, Angelou distrusts everyone, especially Whites. Nonetheless, she is repeatedly surprised by the kindness and goodwill of many Whites she meets, and, thus, her suspicions begin to soften into understanding.

The second test comes when she meets Tosh, a White man of Greek descent, who visits the record shop regularly and reveals, through his selection of records, that he is a devotee of Black jazz and blues—of Charlie Parker, Thelonius Monk, Dizzy Gillespie, Max Roach, and Dexter Gordon. Surprised by Tosh's genuine appreciation of the same music that hardcore Black jazz and blues enthusiasts love, Angelou is again placed in a circumstance that forces her to alter her opinion of Whites, although this step does not come easily. She recalls "My brain didn't want to accept the burden of my ears. Was that a white man talking?"[2] Angelou faces a more difficult test when she is forced to make a decision about marrying Tosh, who is courting her through her son, a difficulty that stems from her memory

of her Southern past and from her first-hand experience
with the ugliness of white prejudice:

> . . . that decision had been made for me by the centuries of slav-
> ery. . . . Anger and guilt decided before my birth that Black was
> Black and White was White and although the two might share
> sex, they must never exchange love.[3]

Angelou resolves her dilemma by rationalizing, and thereby
convincing herself, that Tosh

> was Greek, not White American; therefore I needn't feel that I
> had betrayed my race by marrying one of the enemy, nor could
> White Americans believe that I had so forgiven them the past that
> I was ready to love a member of their tribe.[4]

But this does not lessen the discomfort she feels when she
and Tosh are in the presence of other Blacks, nor does it
alleviate the guilt she feels throughout their marriage.

Although Tosh proves to be a good husband and father,
Angelou is forced to surrender her independence for the
security she has yearned for in marriage. This not only
means that she must cater to Tosh's every desire and de-
mand, even limiting her friendships and those of her son to
persons approved by Tosh, but that she must also accept,
without challenge, Tosh's attempts to control their beliefs
about God and religion. But even as Angelou wages her
own silent protest against Tosh by surreptitiously visiting
a different Black church each Sunday morning, she mistakes prison for security, allowing a little more of her independence to be taken away, never challenging the sub-
stance of Tosh's views or demands.

When the marriage finally ends, after two-and-a-half
years, Angelou romanticizes the relationship as she had
always done when relationships ended. She also weeps for
her loss of security, fearing that she and her son

would be thrown again into a maelstrom of rootlessness. Unadmitted was the sense of strangulation I had begun to feel or the insidious quality of guilt for having a white husband, which surrounded me like an evil aura when we were in public.[5]

Yet, the maturity that Angelou gains from the relationship with Tosh and her acceptance of him in marriage teach her tolerance, a quality which she will come to value.

Even so, much later, when three whites—Jorie and Don and Barrie—offer Angelou their friendship freely and wholly, as well as an opportunity to perform at the Purple Onion in San Francisco, she is temporarily disoriented by their openness:

My God. My world was spinning off its axis, and there was nothing to hold on to. Anger and haughtiness, pride and prejudice, my old back-up team, would not serve me in this predicament. These whites were treating me as an equal, as if I could do whatever they could do. They did not consider that race, height, or gender or lack of education might have crippled me and that I should be regarded as someone invalided.[6]

But Angelou is also frank enough to admit some inviting self-indulgence:

Oh, the holiness of always being the injured party. The historically oppressed can find not only sanctity but safety in the state of victimization. When access to a better life has been denied often enough, and successfully enough, one can use the rejection as an excuse to cease all efforts.[7]

Angelou systematically resists the temptation. The friendship that she develops with Jorie, Don, and Barrie—a friendship among peers—is pivotal because it represents a significant step in her movement toward adulthood.

When her marriage ends, a marriage which for a time Angelou describes as "a Good Housekeeping advertisement,"[8] she becomes a dancer among strippers who are obliged to drink with customers in a dingy North Beach nightclub in San Francisco. But out of this comes an engagement at the Purple Onion and her life is changed forever. With her success at the Purple Onion, Angelou is catapulted into another career. Initially, she is offered opportunities to replace Eartha Kitt in *New Faces* and to appear with Pearl Bailey on Broadway in *House of Flowers*. However, she has seen *Porgy and Bess* and has fallen hopelessly in love with the musical. Thus, when she is asked to join the *Porgy and Bess* touring company as a featured dancer, she accepts the offer immediately and is excited by the incredible turn of events that will bring her "from a past of rejection . . . of dead-end streets and culs-de-sac"[9] into the bright sun of Canada, Italy, France, Greece, Yugoslavia, and Egypt. Much of *Singin' and Swingin'*—116 pages of the 269 page work—is Angelou's praisesong to *Porgy*, so much so that the musical emerges almost as an antagonist that enthralls Angelou, beckoning and seducing her away from her responsibilities, yet teaching her significant lessons, which expand her education beyond the familiar circle of community and family. Angelou's travels with *Porgy and Bess* throw her into contact with people of many nationalities and classes, some of whom have never before seen a Black person, and expand and complicate her understanding of the complexities of race relations. One of the most revealing aspects of the work is the human experiences a Black American finds traveling in the world.

In Montreal, for example, Angelou recalls the stories of slaves escaping by underground railroad to Canada, and she feels a kinship with the people she sees in the streets. Angelou writes:

Among the many perversities in American race relations is the fact that Blacks do not relish looking closely at whites. After hundreds of years of being the invisible people ourselves, as soon as many of us have achieved economic security we try to force whites into nonexistence by ignoring them.

Montreal provided me with my first experience of looking freely at whites. The underground railroad had had Canada as its final destination, and slaves had created a powerful liturgy praising Canada which was sung all over the world. Spirituals abounded with references to the Biblical body of water, the River Jordan. I had been told that Jordan, in our music, meant the Mississippi or the Arkansas or the Ohio River and the stated aim to get to Canaan land was the slave's way of saying he longed to go to Canada for freedom.

Therefore, Canadians were exempt from many Blacks' rejection of whites. They were another people. I observed their clean streets and the fact that their faces did not tighten when they saw me. The atmosphere was comfortable enough to allow me to try my recently learned French words. Sometimes I was understood.[10]

In Italy, crowds push in around Angelou and in their broken English speak the name Joe Louis, and she communicates beyond language barriers to the hearts of the Italian people.

As Angelou learns lessons, she shares them with the reader. When, for example, she is asked to sing at an elegant reception by a Parisienne, Angelou invites two Senegalese men to escort her, and all three are snubbed by the hostess. While the hostess is willing to be gracious to a Black American performer, she cannot—will not—extend the same courtesy to French Africans. This is a rude awakening for Angelou, who reflects:

Paris was not a place for me or my son. The French could entertain the idea of me because they were not immersed in guilt about a mutual history—just as white Americans found it easier to accept Africans, Cubans, or South American Blacks than Blacks who had lived with them foot to neck for two hundred years. I saw no benefit in exchanging one kind of prejudice for another.[11]

Later in Belgrade, Angelou becomes the object of fear and curiosity to an old couple who had never seen a Black person; but on the streets of Zagreb, crowds press around her chanting the name Paul Robeson and singing "Deep River" in husky, piping voices. Angelou comments on this moving experience.:

I stood in the dusty store and considered my people, our history and Mr. Paul Robeson. Somehow, the music fashioned by men and women out of an anguish they could describe only in dirges was to be a passport for me and their other descendants into far and strange lands and long unsure futures.

> "Oh, don't you want to go
> To that gospel feast?"

I added my voice to the melody:

> "That promised land
> Where all is peace?"

I made no attempt to wipe away the tears. I could not claim a forefather who came to America on the *Mayflower*. Nor did any ancestor of mine amass riches to leave me free from toil. My great-grandparents were illiterate when their fellow men were signing the Declaration of Independence, and the first families of my people were bought separately and sold apart, nameless and without traces—yet there was this:

> "Deep River
> My home is over Jordan."

I had a heritage, rich and nearer than the tongue which gives it voice. My mind resounded with the words and my blood raced to the rhythms:

> "Deep River
> I want to cross over into campground." [12]

In Egypt, when Angelou visits the pyramids and observes a Pharoanic Tomb rising above her head, she becomes even more reflective:

Israelites and Nubians and slaves from Carthage and Mesopotamia had built it, sweating, bleeding, and finally dying for the mass of stones which would become in the twentieth century no more than the focus for tourists' cameras.

My grandmother had been a member of a secret Black American female society, and my mother and father were both active participants in the Masons and Eastern Star organizations. Their symbols which I found hidden in linen closets and night stands, were drawings of the Pyramid at Giza, or Cheops' tomb. [13]

Meshed between these moving, but often disconcerting experiences, are the joy, frustration, and tension of being a member of a touring company, and the struggle to come to grips with the disparity between the company members' stage and private lives. Ultimately, she comes face-to-face with the disillusioning truth that art is artifice, and reluctantly she learns to cope with "the papier-mache world of great love, passion and poignancy." [14] Even so, Angelou's travels and experiences with *Porgy and Bess*, particularly her visit to Africa, do much to enhance her maturity and her feelings of self-worth. The triumph of the opera company is not only the dramatic success of a talented company of Black artists, but it is also the triumphal blooming of a talented, determined young Black woman into the adult self and into a fully liberated person.

The thread which binds this retrospective account of the emerging self is, however, much stronger than the themes of racial identity or personal liberation. Angelou's love for her son and the guilty conflict she experiences over having left him to join the *Porgy and Bess* company overshadow her other experiences. The saddest part of *Singin' and Swingin'* is the young Guy, who, though deeply loved by Angelou, seems to be shoved into the background whenever a need to satisfy her monetary requirements or theatrical ambitions arises.

In the end, Angelou resists the temptation of Europe and Africa and returns to America, where she will affirm and renew her love for her son. She finds him unhappy and withdrawn and, as a consequence, is driven almost to suicide by guilt and self-reproachment. However, she and her son are able to survive the crisis and to emerge with a surer sense of the strong bond of love between them. While *Singin' and Swingin'* is certainly a praisesong to *Porgy and Bess*, it is also a love song to Angelou's son, who grows up over the course of its pages. One cares very much about this intelligent, sensitive boy who decides, at the age of nine, to change his name from Clyde to Guy, just as Angelou had changed from Marguerite to Maya and had accepted the show business change of *Angelous* to *Angelou* at a time when she needed a new beginning. Throughout the work, one sympathizes also with Angelou in her maternal angst—ambivalently wrestling with guilt for leaving her son to sing and swing with *Porgy and Bess*, yet needing the freedom and the space such a tour gave her to expand both intellectually and psychologically.

For Angelou, autobiography continues to serve as a way of enabling her to contemplate the most painful and terrifying aspects of existence and as a way of celebrating those things she values most highly in life. Family, home, music, faith, friends, and knowledge are the cornerstones of this life. When one meets Maya Angelou in her story, one encounters the humor, the pain, the exuberance, the honesty, and the determination of a human being who has experienced life fully and retained her strong sense of self.

Both the writing and the story fulfill the promise of the title. Angelou has a remarkable ability to recreate scenes from her life. In narrating retrospective accounts of incidents and dialogue, there is necessarily some contrivance, but there is always the ring of authenticity in the telling.

The Heart of a Woman, the fourth volume in the autobiographical series, follows Angelou through the late fifties and early sixties, a transitional time between national eras, of Little Rock, of Black American firsts in sports, of spirited turmoil in the United States Congress over the passage of the Civil Rights Commission's Voting Rights Bill. It is the period when Laurel Canyon was the official residential area of Hollywood—a time when, although the few Blacks who lived there were rich, famous, and fair-skinned enough to pass (i.e., Billy Eckstein, Billy Daniels, Herb Jeffries), most Black Americans could not rent or buy the modest bungalows there without recourse to White go-betweens. It is a time when Billy Holiday is still alive and, in a rare moment, sings "Strange Fruit" to Angelou's precocious son.

A multiple chronicle, *The Heart of a Woman* charts the fiery upheaval of those years (1957–1962) and the ups and downs of Angelou's own life, changes that include her introduction to the society and world of Black artists and writers; careers as actress, editor, and activist; her involvement in the Harlem Writers' Guild and the publication of her first short story; a marriage to a South African freedom fighter and their life together in New York, London, and Cairo; and the rearing of a teen-age son.

Beginning with the lines from a spiritual, "The ole ark's

a-moverin', a-moverin', a-moverin'; the ole Ark's a-moverin' along,"[15] Angelou observes that the ancient spiritual could have been the theme song of the United States in 1957, for

We were a-moverin' to, fro, up, down, and often in concentric circles.

We created a maze of contradictions. Black and White Americans danced a fancy and often dangerous do-si-do. In our steps forward, and our abrupt turns, sharp spins and reverses, we became our own befuddlement.[16]

For Angelou, the old ark is indeed "a-moverin' along." Early on in this volume and to Guy's sadness over yet another disruption that will bring about unwanted changes in his life, Angelou moves to New York where, under the influence of John and Grace Killens, Abbey Lincoln and Max Roach, Lorraine Hansberry, James Baldwin, Paule Marshall and other Blacks who are doing important work, she begins to change. Angelou begins to acquire a new sense of Black dignity and to become more politicized, growing more aware than ever before that Black people in Harlem, as throughout the country, are changing, "that the echo of African drums is less distant . . . than it had been for over a century."[17] Increasingly, Angelou realizes that the changes in Harlem are symbolic of the changes Blacks are making everywhere:

One hundred and twenty-fifth street was to Harlem what the Mississippi was to the South, a long travelling river always going somewhere, carrying something. A furniture store offering gaudy sofas and fake leopard-skin chairs shouldered Mr. Micheaux's book shop, which prided itself on having or being able to get a copy of any book written by a black person since 1900. It was true that sportily dressed fops stood on 125th and Seventh Avenue saying, "Got horse for the course and coke for the hope," but across the street, conservatively dressed men told concerned crowds of the satanic nature of whites and the divinity of Elijah Muhammad. Black men and women had begun to wear multi-colored African prints. They moved through Harlem like bright sails on a dark sea.

I also know that fewer people giggled or poked the sides of their neighbors when they noticed my natural hair style.

Clever appliance-store owners left their TV sets on the channels broadcasting UN affairs. I had seen Black people standing in front of the stores watching the faces of international diplomats. Although no sound escaped into the streets, the attentive crowds appeared. I had waited with a group of strangers one night near St. Nicholas Avenue. The mood was hopeful, as if a promise was soon to be kept.[18]

Although Angelou continues her singing career in small clubs on the Lower East Side of New York and later enjoys a successful appearance at the Apollo Theatre in Harlem, she takes a major step towards assuring her own personal liberation and freedom:

I made the decision to quit show business. Give up the skintight dresses and manicured smiles. The false concern over sentimental lyrics. I would never again work to make people smile . . . [but] would take on the responsibility of making them think. Now was the time to demonstrate my own seriousness.[19]

While her decision to end her show business career is partly political, Angelou is not yet involved in organized politics. This involvement comes later when, for the first time, she goes to hear Martin Luther King, Jr. speak. King, who has recently been released from a Birmingham jail, is in New York to raise money for the Southern Christian Leadership Conference (SCLC) and to make Northerners aware of the fight being waged in the South. So moved is Angelou by the power of King's commitment that she will co-produce with Godfrey Cambridge the successful *Cabaret for Freedom* at the Village Gate to raise money for the SCLC. Her ability at getting the show on the boards so impresses the SCLC leadership that King appoints Angelou his Northern Coordinator.

Later when she is invited to join the seminal Harlem Writer's Guild, Angelou finds her earliest works torn to shreds after readings, but her entry into Harlem society fires her inner need to commit herself to the Black struggle for freedom. From her perspective as Northern Coordinator for the SCLC, Angelou writes of the fire, spirit, and sometimes idealistic naivete that ignited Harlem when there was no turning back on the road to integration.

The social and cultural history of Black Americans is richly revealed in autobiography, and *The Heart of a Woman* documents the sixties when Angelou engaged actively in political protest with King's organization in New York City. However, in the 1960's, when so much was evolving on the political front, Angelou, disenchanted with the mildness of King's philosophy, becomes more and more attracted to the causes of Black militants—Black American and African—and more committed to activism. Of this Angelou writes:

> Redemptive suffering had always been the part of Martin's argument that I found difficult to accept. I had seen distress fester souls and bend people's bodies out of shape, but I had yet to see anyone redeemed by pain.[20]

Thus, even while she admires King's commitment and integrity, Angelou and her New York friends are drawn to Patrice Lumumba, Kwame Nkrumah, Sekou Touré and Malcolm X, to expatriate South African freedom fighters and to young militants who shout, "Hey Krushchev. Go on, with your bad self,'' when the Soviet leader visits Fidel Castro at Harlem's famous Hotel Teresa.

Angelou and her activist women friends, charged by their new political zeal, organize a group which they name CAWAH, the acronym for the Cultural Association for Women of African Heritage. The organization includes dancers, teachers, singers, writers, and musicians; and its intention is to support all Black civil rights causes. Lumumba's assassination in the Congo sends CAWAH off on a protest demonstration at the United Nations with much of Harlem joining in the demonstration as well as two other pro-Africa groups: The Liberation Committee for Africa and On Guard. Particularly moving is Angelou's alternately frightening and comic account of the demonstration that turns into a near riot. In an angry response to what would become the most memorable interruption of the General Assembly, Adlai Stevenson, U.S. Ambassador to the United Nations, apologizes to the international body. Whitney Young, Director of the Urban League, and Roy Wilkins, National Secretary of the NAACP, proclaim that "the ugly demonstration was carried out by an irresponsible element . . . of the Black community,"[21] but Malcolm X, while strongly rejecting CAWAH's strategy, posits:

> Black people are letting white Americans know that the time is coming for ballots or bullets. They know it is useless to ask their enemy for justice. And surely whites are the enemies of blacks, otherwise how did we get to this country in the first place?[22]

Angelou is not only an observer in this area of protest and hope, but she works with CAWAH, with pro-Africa groups, and with Martin Luther King, Jr. in SCLC; and she comes to believe that, when the final history of the sixties is written, King will be known as one of the great minds of the 20th Century.

While *The Heart of a Woman* documents a period when Angelou, for the first time, becomes an active political protestor, Angelou does not, in retrospect, enlarge her own image as a protestor. In describing one particular staged protest, she recalls, "I had been silly, irresponsible, and unprepared."[23] Such honesty in no way undermines the seriousness of Angelou's commitment to the movement, but it does help readers to understand both the confusion and courage felt by Black activists in a passage in American life which has come to be historic. While the recounting of the sixties is of interest because it enhances the reader's understanding of such men as Malcolm X, Martin Luther King, Jr., and Patrice Lumumba, only Angelou's preoccupation with herself can give the readers the kind of personal history that the autobiography makes so formidable in *The Heart of a Woman*.

At the time of sit-ins and freedom rides and Africa's astonishing birth of nations, it was almost inevitable that there would be a play performed by Blacks to offer some relevant comment on the race issue. The play is Jean Genet's *The Blacks*, and despite her work in SCLC, Angelou finds the time to act in the lead role at the St. Mark's Theater off-Broadway as the White Queen. At first, opposed to acting in a play that portrays Blacks assuming the roles of their former masters, Angelou soon begins to enjoy the catharsis that the play's politics affords her. She comments:

The play was delicious to our taste. We were only acting, but we were black actors in 1960. On that small New York stage, we reflected the real-life confrontations that were occurring daily in America's streets. Whites did live above us, hating and fearing and threatening our existence. Blacks did sneer behind their masks at the rules they both loathed and envied. We would throw off the white yoke which dragged us down into an eternal genuflection.

I started enjoying my role. I used the White Queen to ridicule mean white women and brutal white men who had too often injured me and mine. Every inane posture and haughty attitude I had ever seen found its place in my White Queen.

Genet had been right at last about one thing. Blacks should be used to play whites. For centuries we had probed their faces, the angles of their bodies, the sounds of their voices and even their odors. Often our survival had depended upon the accurate reading of a white man's chuckle or the disdainful wave of a white woman's hand. Whites, on the other hand, always knew that no serious penalty threatened them if they misunderstood blacks. Whites were safely isolated from our concerns. When they chose, they could lift the racial curtain which separated us. They could indulge in sexual escapades, increase our families with mulatto bastards, make fortunes out of our music and eunuchs out of our men, then in seconds they could step away, and return unscarred to their pristine security. The cliche of whites being ignorant of blacks was not only true, but understandable. Oh, but we knew them with the intimacy of a surgeon's scalpel.[24]

The Blacks is not only a brilliant success, but working with the cast is an incredible experience which feeds Angelou's artistic growth. The original cast includes Cicely Tyson, Godfrey Cambridge, Roscoe Lee Brown, James Earl Jones, Jay Flash Riley, Raymond St. Jacques, Cynthia Belgrave, Charles Gordone, Helen Martin, Lou Gossett, Lex Monson, Abbey Lincoln, and Maya Angelou. Nonetheless, Angelou is forced to resign from the play when Sidney Bernstein, the director-producer, refuses to compensate her and actress Ethel Ayler for composing the music for the show when, on the morning of opening night, Max Roach withdraws his compositions from the production. When Angelou insists that she and Miss Ayler must be paid something for composing the music, Bernstein, making no attempt to dilute his scorn, bellows, "Get off my back, will you? You didn't compose anything. I saw you. You just sat down at the piano and made up something."[25] Bernstein's incredulous statement initially paralyzes the movement of Angelou's brain, but she recovers quickly, concluding that she is not locked into *The Blacks* or the St. Mark's Playhouse and, therefore, must resist any exploitation of herself or talent. Recalling this incident, Angelou explains:

> It was ironic that the producer of a play which exposed white greed so eloquently could himself be such a glutton. Whether we were in the mines of South Africa, or the liberal New York theater, nothing changed. Whites wanted everything. They thought they deserved everything. That they wanted to possess all the materials of the earth was in itself disturbing, but that they also wanted to control the souls and the pride of people was inexplicable.[26]

In *The Heart of a Woman*, and in the other volumes of the autobiography as well, Angelou utilizes biographical and historical data to lead the reader away from the time-honored myths and toward a fuller understanding of the historically-bound present. While incorporating social and political issues in her work, she does not allow protest to dominate her writing to the exclusion of other concerns. Instead, she consciously broaches the subjects of survival and social change from a variety of vantage points: artist, activist, woman. Each of Angelou's books, while recounting the story of one individual's fight for survival, extends the perspective of a woman's life in contemporary social and cultural history.

Meanwhile, underneath the excitement of her movement in New York, Angelou feels that something vital is missing in her life as she copes both with Guy, who is becoming increasingly more independent and growing away from her, and with her own physical and emotional needs as a woman. What is most remarkable about Angelou's autobiography is her refusal to withhold anything. Her writing here, describing her longings, doubts, and shortcomings, is raw, bare honesty. Angelou discusses at length her folly at feeling, despite her independence and success, that what she needs to make her life and her son's life complete is a man. Thus, she leaps at the first man who is attentive to her, a bail bondsman, simply because he represents security. But, then, she drops him when she meets Vusumzi Make, a South African freedom fighter whose harrowing escape from South African imprisonment immediately catches her imagination and she his fancy. They marry.

From here, Angelou relates her changing definitions of self as she tries to be the proper wife of a respected African but at the same time realizes that she cannot be the subservient woman her husband wants here to be. She is discomfited by his oftimes patronizing tone in speaking to her "as if [she] were the little shepherd girl and he the Old Man of Kilimanjaro,"[27] and by his expectation that she be not only the perfect African wife and the perfect cook but also the perfect housekeeper. Angelou recalls:

> It seemed to me that I washed, scrubbed, mopped, dusted and waxed thoroughly every other day. Vus was particular. He checked on my progress. Sometimes he would pull the sofa away from the wall to see if possibly I had missed a layer of dust. If he found his suspicions confirmed, his response could wither me. He would drop his eyes and shake his head, his face saddened with disappointment. I wiped down the walls, because dirty fingerprints could spoil his day and ironed his starched shirts (he had his shoes polished professionally).
>
> . . .
>
> I was unemployed but I had never worked so hard in my life.[28]

Angelou and Guy move to Cairo with Make so that he can be closer to his fellow expatriates as he carries on the struggle for Black liberation in South Africa. However, by now a recurring pattern has emerged; Make is not only an energetic womanizer, but he is also irresponsible, failing to pay the rent and other bills. With her will to survive, her independence, and her American gumption, Angelou does the unheard of in Egypt: she goes to work. With the help of her friend David DuBois, Angelou secures a position as associate editor of the English-language *Arab Observer* and teaches herself how to be a "reporter in process."

Working as a journalist in Cairo, Angelou is dismayed by the sexual hostility of Nasser's male revolutionaries and shabbily deceived by Make's improprieties. But her awakening observations in Egypt, coupled with the knowledge she gains from her African and Egyptian friends, show her that, while all Blacks are not the same because of cultural differences, all are brothers and sisters united in the flesh. Before the end of *The Heart of a Woman*, Angelou leaves Make, because she realizes that she can no longer live with him:

> Vus was African and his values were different from mine. Among the people I knew, my family and friends, promiscuity was the ultimate blow in marriage. It struck down the pillars of trust which held the relationship aloft.[29]

As Angelou and Guy travel to a new life in Ghana, Angelou weeps and Guy assures his mother: "It'll be O.K., Mom. Don't cry. I love you, Mom. Lots of people love you."[30] Angelou writes:

> I made no attempt to explain that I was not crying because of a lack of love, certainly not the loss of Vus' affection. I was mourning all my ancestors. I had never felt that Egypt was really Africa, but now that our route had taken us across the Sahara, I could look down from my window seat and see trees, and bushes, rivers and dense forest. It all began here. The jumble of poverty-stricken children sleeping in rat-infested tenements or abandoned cars.

The terrifying moan of my grandmother, "Bread of Heaven, Bread of Heaven, feed me till I want no more." The drugged days and alcoholic nights of men for whom hope had not been born. The loneliness of women who would never know appreciation or a mite's share of honor. Here, there, along the banks of that river, someone was taken, tied with ropes, shackled with chains, forced to march for weeks carrying the double burden of neck irons and abysmal fear. In that large clump of trees, looking like wood moss from the plane's great height, boys and girls had been hunted like beasts, caught and tethered together. Sacrificial lambs on the altar of greed. America's period of orgiastic lynchings had begun on yonder broad savannah.[31]

In the best parts of this volume, Angelou uses the narrative gifts of an accomplished fiction writer. Enhancing all of this story-telling power are her great humor and her impeccably accurate ear for voices and dialogue: her stark encounter with Billy Holiday; meeting her mother at the Desert Hotel in Fresno soon after it is integrated; her last appearance at the Apollo Theater when the audience joins, protects, and celebrates her; her first meeting with Malcolm X, following the demonstration of CAWAH at the UN; her rowdy escape from her indignant husband at an ambassador's party at the Waldorf Astoria; and the West African palaver in Cairo to debate publicly her decision to end her marriage to Make. In each of these scenes, as throughout the work, Angelou's prose is sculpted, concise, rich with flavor and surprise, exuding a natural confidence and command. A fine example of this imaginative prose is Angelou's description of an evening with Make when they first meet:

At the dining table he spread before me the lights and shadows of Africa. Glories stood in thrilling array. Warrior queens, in necklaces of blue and white beads led armies against marauding Europeans. Nubile girls danced in celebrations of the victories of Shaka, the Zulu King. The actual earth of Africa was "black and strong like the girls back home: and glinted with gold and diamonds. African men covered their betrothed with precious stones and specially woven cloth. He asked me to forgive the paucity of the gift he had for me and to understand that when we returned to Mother Africa he would adorn me with riches the like of which I had never imagined. When he led me into the darkened guest room and placed a string of beads around my neck, all my senses were tantalized. I would have found the prospect of a waterless month in the Sahara not only exciting, but acceptable. The amber beads on my nut-brown skin caught fire. I looked into the mirror and saw exactly what I wanted him to see: a young African virgin, made beautiful for the chief.[32]

There are themes in *The Heart of a Woman*, most begun in the earlier volumes of the autobiography, which critics will continue to explore: Angelou's movement between reality and fantasy; the way Angelou, the autobiographer, records and alters events; the passage from innocence to knowledge; and the moments of decision and indecision. But the singular power of the work is the authority Angelou wields over her own life, and the sense of almost heroic continuity her autobiography gives. Through her childhood with her grandmother in Stamps, Arkansas, her career as a dancer in *Porgy and Bess*, her work with Martin Luther King, Jr., her marriage to a South African freedom fighter, and her life as a journalist in Cairo, the themes of survival, humanity, injustice, and family strength, interwoven with optimism and humor, never leave her. Angelou's belief in continuity is perhaps strengthened, paradoxically, by the fact that she has been on the move most of her life—from Arkansas to California, Stamps to St. Louis and back to Stamps, and Mexico from New York to Egypt and Ghana, from London to San Francisco, from the Pacific Palisades to Winston-Salem, North Carolina.

The Heart of a Woman is unlike the earlier volumes of the autobiography. The universal message of triumph over suffering that triumphed in *Caged Bird* and *Gather Together* is still present, but it is subtly buried under her growing awareness of what it means to a Black American in the United States in the early sixties.

In *Singin' and Swingin' and Gettin' Merry Like Christmas* and *The Heart of a Woman*, Angelou provides memorable portraits of the evolution of a young Black woman and of the adult self in bloom.

5

Redefining the Self Through Place and Culture

"Swing low, sweet chariot,
Coming for to carry me home."

—from the Negro Spiritual

"The ache for home lives in all of us, the safe place where we
can go as we are and not be questioned."
          —Maya Angelou, *All God's Children Need Traveling Shoes*

In *All God's Children Need Traveling Shoes,* the fifth
volume in her personal chronicle, Maya Angelou proves
conclusively that she is a master of the autobiographical
form in which the personal statement transcends the self in
such a way that the self becomes the representation of the
people, and the people find a voice in the self.[1] While this
work continues to enrich the traditions of retrospective
writing of Black Americans, in this latest volume, Angelou
departs from the primary focus of Black American autobiography which involves the confrontation of the Black
self with a society that threatens to destroy it. In her earlier

volumes, Angelou recaptures that confrontation, while at the same time, portraying the extraordinary life of a Black woman who has survived and triumphed.

In *All God's Children Need Traveling Shoes,* (hereafter referred to as *Traveling Shoes*), Angelou takes the reader to Ghana, West Africa, during the early 1960s, where she tries to forge links with her past. In this volume, Angelou not only relates the personal journey of a Black American woman in search of a home, but she also touches upon the personal journeys of other Black American expatriates searching for an African home as well. In doing so, she records the history of a generation of American expatriates in Africa in no less a way than Ernest Hemingway and Henry James record the history of American expatriates in Europe. Like Angelou, as one critic has observed, both James and Hemingway deal with individuals in search of self, men and women who are seeking some longed-for-entity that they cannot find in their motherland, and who fail to find what they are searching for in their adopted land. Gertrude Stein's term, "a lost generation," applies to the world of Angelou's Black American expatriates as much as it did to White American expatriates in Europe of the 1920s.[2]

In *Traveling Shoes,* readers are reminded that, in the late 1950s, Africa was for many Black Americans their first opportunity to identify in a positive way with their ancestral home. Instead of looking away from Africa, numerous Black American men and women began to look at it. Familiar feelings of indifference, rejection and shame began to be replaced by feelings of interest, acceptance and pride. This change began to manifest itself with the approach of independence in Ghana and the emergence of Kwame Nkrumah as the first new African world leader, followed by other new African states and the appearance of other

African Black men and women in places of power. What Black Americans gleaned from these events was not only the spectacle of defeated White power but the more gloriously gratifying image of Blacks in positions of leadership, commanding attention and respect. Ordinary Afro-Americans, through their newspapers, radios and televisions, were introduced to a succession of African dignitaries: Lumumba, Kenyatta, Mboya, Touré, Nyerere, Balewa, Senghor, Houphouet-Boigny. From the late fifties through much of the sixties, Africa, as symbolized by these distinguished African visitors who were achieving national and international visibility, offered Black Americans a new place in history. Moreover, it offered them a new link to their past and a new awareness of their historic continuity.[3] Thus, *Travelling Shoes,* in recapturing this mood, is a mixture of Maya Angelou's personal recollection and a historical documentation of the time in which it is set.

What was to have been for Angelou a short visit in Accra, en route to her new home in Liberia, becomes a three-year stay when Guy, who is now a teenager and ready for college, is seriously injured in a nearly fatal automobile accident. Angelou's explicit purpose in coming to Accra was to enroll Guy in the University of Ghana, one of the most respected institutions in West Africa. Although she had planned to move to Liberia, where a job awaited her, she is forced to remain in Ghana until Guy recovers. Underneath the articulated reasons, are, however, other impulses which have brought Angelou to this place: the need to leave Egypt, following her broken marriage to Vusumzi Make, and her decision to bring up her son in a country of Blacks governed by Blacks. When Angelou is unable to forgive the drunken man who has caused the accident and nearly robbed her only child of his future, she turns her grief and anger inward, neglecting herself in many ways. But she is saved by her friend Julian Mayfield, who provides a much-needed reality check. He advises:

> You need to have someone, a woman to talk to you. . . . Some-body needs to tell you that you have to give up this self-pity. You're letting yourself go. Look at your clothes. Look at your hair. Hell, it's Guy whose neck was broken. Not yours. . . . Everybody understands . . . as much as anyone can understand another's pain . . . but you've forgotten to be polite. Hell, girl, everybody feels sorry for you, but nobody owes you a damn thing. You know that. Don't forget your background. Your mother didn't raise you in a dog house.[4]

Following his tough but gentle counsel, Mayfield introduces Angelou to Efua Sutherland—poet, teacher, playwright, and Director of the National Theatre of Ghana—recounting Angelou's tragic story. Afterwards, Sutherland, in an encouraging, sisterly gesture, places her hand on Angelou's cheek and comforts her with these words:

> Sister, you have need of a sister friend because you need to weep, and you need someone to watch you while you weep.[5]

Up to this moment, Angelou has "slept, awakened, walked, and lived in a thick atmosphere, which has only allowed shallow breathing and routine behavior,"[6] but Sutherland's quiet support frees her to cry out all the bitterness and self-pity of the past days. Through this sanctioned outpouring, Angelou loses herself in order to find herself. Afterwards, Sutherland takes Angelou to her home where she introduces her to her children as their Auntie Maya, and where they spend their evening eating and drinking and talking about the great writers—Shakespeare, Langston Hughes, Alexander Pope, and Sheridan.

As Guy heals and later begins his studies at the University of Ghana, Angelou begins to explore her growing relationship to the land of her ancestors and is "soon swept into an adoration for Ghana as a young girl falls in love, heedless and with slight chance of finding the emotion requited."[7] In many ways, Guy's accident is fortuitous, for Angelou is in search of both home and place; and in those glory days of Kwame Nkrumah, she will discover that Ghana is the center of an African cultural renaissance. Unlike Liberia, which was founded by former American slaves, Ghana is culturally African. The early 1960s is a period of cultural rebirth—a time of pride in old values and new freedom, a time of promise and growth.

The attraction to Ghana is both symbolic and cultural, for, like many Blacks, Angelou perceives it to be a lost homeland. She writes:

> So I had finally come home. The prodigal child, having strayed, been stolen or sold from the land of her fathers, having squandered her mother's gifts and having laid down in cruel gutters, had at last arisen and directed herself back to the welcoming arms of the family where she would be bathed, clothed with fine raiment and seated at the welcoming table.[8]

Angelou is one of the nearly two hundred Black Americans from St. Louis, New York City, Washington, D.C., Los Angeles, San Francisco, Atlanta, and Dallas, who has come to Ghana in the hope of living out the Biblical Story. For these Black American expatriates, Ghana is not only the home of Kwame Nkrumah but also the fountainhead of Pan Africanism—the long-held dream of a united and powerful mother continent and a world community of sons and daughters of Africa wherever they happened to be. It was the dream of Alexander Crummell, Martin R. Delaney, and Edward W. Blyden; of Marcus Garvey, George Padmore and W.E.B. DuBois. It is now the dream of Malcolm X, Julian Mayfield, Alphaeus Hunton, and Maya Angelou.

Angelou is captured by the sights and sounds of Ghana, but more deeply by the Ghanaian people who remind her of her Arkansas and California pasts:

> Their skins were the colors of my childhood cravings: peanut butter, licorice, chocolate, caramel. Theirs was the laughter of home, quick and without artifice. The erect and graceful walk of the women reminded me of my Arkansas Grandmother, Sunday-hatted, on her way to church. I listened to men talk, and whether or not I understood their meaning, there was a melody as familiar as sweet potato pie, reminding me of my Uncle Tommy Baxter in Santa Monica, California.[9]

As is true in the earlier volumes of her autobiography, Angelou's style is primarily episodic. With a fine eye for descriptive details and an ear for anecdote, Angelou tells many stories within the larger story, while focusing on her major theme of a Black American's search for home. Thus, she skillfully describes the similarities and differences between Africans and Black Americans through her vivid portrayals of ordinary people such as her Ghanaian hair stylist; the elderly steward in the Senior Common Room of the University of Ghana; and of the more privileged men and women like Professor J.H. Nketia, one of Ghana's most respected scholars; Poet Kwesi Brew; Nana Nketsia, the first African Vice-Chancellor of the University of Ghana; Sheikhali, the exotic Malian importer; Grace Nuamah, the National dancer; and other Ghanaian women with whom she becomes sister-friends. Because Angelou includes stories of both ordinary people and important African dignitaries, the reader gets a sense of Ghanaian society and of the autobiographer's perceptions as a Black American woman who is linked to Africans by race and culture.[10]

One of the most memorable scenes in the autobiography—one in which Angelou writes movingly about the cultural bonds between Africans and Black Americans—is the scene in which she describes the family of Kojo, the "small boy" whom she and her housemates have engaged as an assistant to their steward. One day, Kojo's family, led by his great-grandfather, travel by lorry from Akwapin to Accra, a distance of approximately forty miles, to "bring thanks" to Angelou and her housemates. The very act symbolizes the family's love for and pride in the young Kojo. Angelou describes the family:

> By their bearing, clothes, and jewelry, it was evident that Kojo's family was high-born and well-to-do. If they had travelled from Akwapin by lorry to thank me, it was also clear that they treasured the boy.[11]

After the family has gathered in a formal circle in the living room—the older members seated, the younger ones leaning against the walls—the family elder speaks on behalf of the group, saying, "Auntie, we have family here in town, but none has the Brioni education."[12] In Akan languages, Brioni means White. He continues:

> Our chief and our grandfather told us that if Kojo was to become better, he must have that understanding. Now we have talked to his headmaster. We have spoken to his teachers, and we have listened to your steward who is our cousin. Without payment and without knowing his family, you, Auntie, and your Sisters are teaching our Kojo the Brioni ways of thinking, and so. . . .[13]

The Elder then orders the younger relatives to "bring the thanks." The youngsters bring in crates of vegetables, one after the other, filled with garden eggs, onions, plantain, pineapples, cassava, yam, coco yam, mango, and other West African delicacies. When these gifts have been carefully placed around the room, he continues:

> We want you to know that Kojo did not come from the ground like grass. He has risen like the banyan tree. He has roots, thank you. . . . Kojo's family has many farms, Auntie. . And while we are not trying to repay you and your Sisters, every month we will send you thanks according to the season.[14]

This brief, arduous visit leads Angelou further on her search for Africa. When the group leaves, she reclines on her bed, drinking for herself and for all the nameless orphans of Africa who had been shunted around the world. Her grief and despair are obvious:

> I drank and admitted to a boundless envy of those who remained on the continent, out of fortune or perfidy. Their countries had been exploited and their cultures had been discredited by colonialism. Nonetheless, they could reflect through their priests and chiefs on centuries of continuity. The lowliest could call the name of ancestors who lived centuries earlier. The land upon which they lived had been in their people's possession beyond remembered time. Despite political bondage and economic exploitation, they had retained an ineradicable innocence.

> I doubted if I, or any Black from the diaspora, could really return to Africa. We wore skeletons of old despair like necklaces, heralding our arrival, and we were branded with cynicism. . . . It had often been said that Black people were childish, but in America we had matured without ever experiencing the true abandon of adolescence. Those actions which appeared to be childish most often were exhibitions of bravado, not unlike humming a jazz tune while walking into a gathering of the Ku Klux Klan.

> I drank the gin and ignored the tea [that Kojo brought].[15]

A careful examination of African values, transmitted through generations, provides Angelou with new insights about herself as an individual and as a Black American.

Angelou reexperiences this "boundless envy" when, for the first time, she watches a poor, uneducated servant in Africa react with contemptuous indifference to the callous incivility of White professors at the University of Ghana and ignore their display of "established White rudeness":

> No Black American I had ever known knew that security. Our tenure in the United States, though long and very hard-earned, was always so shaky, we had developed patience as a defense, but never as aggression.[16]

Everyday experiences serve as links to Angelou's past and thus embody powerful meanings. Adopting a Ghanian hairstyle enables her to exorcise the painful memory of Blacks cursing each other on New York City subways or snubbing women in the street throughout the United States who dared to reveal their Negro-ness, because

> They felt betrayed, as if the women wearing the frizzy coiffure were giving away secrets; as if they were letting White folks know that our hair wasn't naturally straight.[17]

In Ghana, Angelou derives many personal truths: the cultural restraints that keep her from being truly African, the severe impact of slavery on the Black American psyche, and her own prejudice. Recalling an unpleasant airlines trip to Berlin on Lufthansa, the heavy German-accented English of the stewardesses, and the black and white photographs she had once seen of emaciated human beings rescued from Auschwitz, she reflects:

> In Ghana I worked hard at forgiving those African chiefs who collaborated in the slave trade centuries before, but couldn't find it in my heart to exonerate the stewardesses who were toddlers at the time of the Holocaust. Prejudice is a burden which confuses the past, threatens the future, and renders the present inaccessible.[18]

Angelou also discovers the inherent contradiction of being

Black yet American. This dichotomy is understood after an assassination attempt is made on President Nkrumah's life and the Black American expatriates are suspected of being conspirators in the crime. While none of the Black expatriates are directly accused and, therefore, continue to be grateful to be in the Motherland, the experience alters them in small ways, making them somewhat less giddy, somewhat less certain of their "place" in Ghana. Even so, Angelou and her compatriots continue to share a kind of collective infatuation with Ghana and Ghanaians, although the Black Americans (except for the chosen few) are ignored or excluded by their African hosts.

It takes many months for Angelou to realize that her own delight in her ancestral homeland is not reciprocated, that Ghana is not the gloryland she expected. Reluctantly, she is forced to admit that the familiar race discrimination of America is replaced by African bias and hostility against American outsiders. An unexpected confrontation with a hostile receptionist at the Ghana Broadcasting Company evokes this comment:

> Was it possible that I and all American Blacks had been wrong on other occasions? Could the cutting treatment we often experienced have been stimulated by something other than our features, our hair and color? Was the odor of old slavery so obvious that people were offended and lashed out at us automatically? Had what we judged as racial prejudice less to do with race and more to do with our particular ancestors' bad luck at having been caught, sold and driven like beasts?

> The receptionist and I could have been sisters, or in fact, might be cousins far removed. Yet her scorn was no different from the supercilious rejections of Whites in the United States. . . . The questions temporarily sobered my intoxication with Africa. For a few days, I examined whether in looking for a home, I and all the emigres were running from a bitter truth that rode lightly but forever at home on our shoulders.[19]

Through this experience, Angelou discovers that being Black in a Black country has its own frustrations. Whether she likes it or not, she begins to discover that she is a Black American, and that in Africa she is a Black American in exile.

As Angelou attempts to define herself and her aspirations against her preconceptions of Africa as Motherland, she is forced to confront her expectations, as well as those of others, thus gaining insight into herself and her compatriots. Gradually she becomes aware of the naivety of their expectations, thereby realizing that Africa provides escape but not redemption.

A most compelling scene is Angelou's description of her visit to Berlin where she introduces a Jewish friend from Israel to a former Nazi and is appalled by the carefully veiled exchange of mutual disdain. When Angelou recounts this incident to Roscoe Lee Brown, actor and close friend, he warns her: "The Israeli knew and you should have known what would happen. Be careful, dear girl, that Africa doesn't take away all your cynicism."[20]

As personal history, *Traveling Shoes* is richly significant in what it records about W.E.B. DuBois, Shirley Graham, and, more significantly, for what it reveals about Angelou's growing confrontation with her double-consciousness: her American and African selves. In response to the August 27, 1963, March on Washington, the Black American community, together with a group of Ghanaians sympathetic to their cause, support the Washington March with a demonstration at the U. S. Embassy in Accra. Having begun their march at midnight to parallel the early morning start in Washington, the demonstrators jeer when two soldiers— one Black—come out the embassy door carrying a folded American flag and proceed to raise the banner at dawn. Although these "Revolutionist Returnees" mock the cer-

emony, they are torn within themselves. Angelou recalls
this moment in one of the most moving and revealing passages of the work:

> As the flag ascended, our jeering increased. A careful listener
> could have heard new vehemence in our shouts. We were scorn-
> ing the symbol of hypocrisy and hope. Many of us had begun to
> realize in Africa that the Stars and Stripes was our flag and our
> only flag, and that knowledge was almost too painful to bear. We
> could physically return to Africa, find jobs, learn languages, even
> marry and remain on African soil all our lives, but we were born
> in the United States and it was the United States which had re-
> jected, enslaved, exploited, then denied us. It was the United
> States which held the graves of our grandmothers and grandfath-
> ers. It was in the United States, under conditions too bizarre to
> detail, that those same ancestors had worked and dreamed of "a
> better day, by and by." There we had learned to live on the head
> of burnt matches, and sleep in holes in the ground. In Arkansas
> and Kansas and Chattanooga, Tennessee, we had decided to be
> no man's creature. In Dallas we put our shoulders to the wheel,
> and our hands in God's hand in Tulsa. We had learned the power
> in Chicago, and met in Detroit insatiable greed. We had our first
> loves in the corn brakes of Mississippi; in the cotton fields of
> Georgia we experienced the thundering pleasure of sex; and on
> 125th Street and 7th Avenue in Harlem the Holy Spirit called us
> to be His own.
>
> I shuddered to think that while we wanted that flag dragged into
> the mud and sullied beyond repair, we also wanted it pristine, its
> white stripes, summer cloud white. Watching it wave in the breeze
> of a distance made us nearly choke with emotion. It lifted us up
> with its promise and broke our hearts with denial.
>
> We hurled invectives against the soldiers' retreating backs, know-
> ing that the two young men were not our enemies and that our
> sneers did not hide our longing for full citizenship under that now
> undulating flag.[21]

News of the death of Dr. W.E.B. DuBois reaches the
demonstrators and their response gives to the event both

a deeply felt sadness and a spirit of renewed commitment. As they march and sing, "Oh, Freedom, Oh, Freedom, Oh, Freedom over me," they see through their minds' eyes the "picture of a dapper little man . . . who earned a Harvard doctorate before the end of the 1800s and who said in 1904, 'The problem of the twentieth century will be the problem of the color line.' "[22]

The autobiographer's memory also documents and recalls events surrounding Angelou's meeting with Malcolm X and provides a lucid portrait of the man and his philosophy. When Angelou met Malcolm X two years earlier, he was "the bombastic spokesman for Elijah Muhammad's Nation of Islam,"[23] who proudly proclaimed from street corners and television screens that Whites were "blue-eyed devils" and that America was guilty of "totalitarian genocide." In Ghana, much to her surprise, Angelou meets a man who is expansive and open, a man who is learning, a man who is no longer in love with a position but in love with truth:

> "I have had to rethink a number of things." He said that though his basic premise that the United States was a racist country held true, he no longer believed that all Whites were devils, nor that any human being was inherently cruel at birth.[24]

The trip to Mecca has transformed many aspects of Malcolm X's philosophical stance, including his theology of race. He explains:

> On this journey to Mecca, I met White men with blue eyes, whom I can call brother with conviction. That means that I am forced to reconsider statements I have made in the past and I must have the courage to speak up and out about these reconsiderations.[25]

Malcolm knew that his new views concerning race would

intensify the already publicized anger of the followers of Elijah Muhammad towards him, but he was convinced that Black Americans were in dire need of truth and that he would continue to speak truth, as he understood it, to the people. Yet the new Malcolm X generously credits his former leader for what he has become:

> The teaching of the honorable Elijah Muhammad enabled me to break the noose that ignorance and racism put around my neck, and I will always thank Allah and the Honorable Elijah Muhammad for that. But a person must make the effort to learn, and growing is the inevitable reward of learning.[26]

Towards the end of his visit in Ghana when Maya lashes out angrily about Shirley DuBois's lack of identity with the Black American struggle, her isolation from the people, and her pride in sitting in the catbird seat in Ghana,'' Malcolm at first chides Maya about her "childish, dangerously immature" outburst and then encourages her to broaden her thinking:

> We need people on each level to fight our battle. Don't be in such a hurry to condemn a person because he doesn't do what you do, or think as you think or as fast. There was a time when you didn't know what you know today. . . . When you hear that the Urban League or the NAACP is giving a formal at the Waldorf-Astoria, I know that you won't go, but don't knock them. They give scholarships to poor Black children. One of those recipients might become a Julian Mayfield, or a Maya Angelou, or a Malcolm X. . . .[27]

Following his return to the United States, Malcolm writes Maya from New York:

> I hope that you will get this letter before James Farmer arrives. The Afro-American community there should not shun him but

should encircle him and make sure that he is exposed to the right kind of thinking . . . to the most undiluted African thinking.[28]

Towards the end of *Traveling Shoes,* Angelou examines her ambiguous feeling about "going home" and faces painful truths about slavery and Black betrayal, and about the joys and disappointments of living in Ghana. Despite her determination to fit into Ghanaian culture, she is homesick and decides that it is time to return to the United States and to *home:*

> If the heart of Africa still remained elusive, my search for it had brought me closer to understanding myself and other human beings. The ache for home lives in all of us, the safe place where we can go as we are and not be questioned. It impels mighty ambitions and dangerous capers. We amass great fortunes at the cost of our souls, or risk our lives in drug dens from London's Soho, to San Francisco's Haight-Ashbury. We shout in Baptist churches, wear yarmulkes and wigs and argue even the tiniest points in the Torah, or worship the sun and refuse to kill cows for the starving. Hoping that by doing these things, home will forget our awful yearning for it.
>
> My mind was made up. I would go back to the United States as soon as possible.[29]

While all of Angelou's work reflects an awareness of her own personal journey from ignorance to enlightenment, *All God's Children Need Traveling Shoes* represents the autobiographer's very conscious awareness of that transition.

6

The Significance of Maya Angelou in Black Autobiographical Tradition

When you truly possess all you have been and done . . . you are fierce with reality.

—Florida Scott-Maxwell
The Measure of My Days

Frequent self-examination is the duty and prudence of all that would know themselves, or would not lose themselves.

—Cotton Mather
Bonifacius: An Essay Upon the Good

What does one mean when one speaks of a Black autobiographical tradition?

Like American autobiography in general, Black American autobiography has great variety. There are, for example, the *Autobiography of Omar Ibn Seid, Slave in North Carolina* (1831), the only known Black slave in America who wrote his life story in Arabic; the classic story of Sojourner Truth (1850) as women's rights defender, temperance partisan, and towering champion of the anti-slavery cause; the accommodationist writings of Booker T. Washington (*Up from Slavery*, 1901) and Jane Edna Hunter (*A Nickel and a Prayer*, 1940), whose autobiographies encouraged other Blacks to follow the philosophy of social accommodation, often convincing themselves that it was the only hope of salvation for the Black masses; and, the autobiographies of James Weldon Johnson (*Along This Way*, 1933) and Mary Church Terrell (*A Colored Woman in a White World*, 1940), which followed a pattern combining the middle-class success story, racial vindication, and social commentary, rather than the strict delineation of personality. There are also Zora Neale Hurston's *Dust Tracks on a Road* (1940), James Baldwin's *Nobody Knows My Name* (1961), and Julius Lester's *Search for the New Land* (1965), which not only represent something new in Black American autobiography of the period in which they were written but also emphasize the writers' determination to discover and to be themselves.

Despite this variety in content and theme, the earliest Black American autobiographies established certain prototypal patterns, both with respect to theme and structure, that recur again and again in later Black autobiographies. The journey to a distant goal, the return home, and the quest which involves the voyage out, achievement, and return are typical patterns in Black autobiography. As noted earlier, one critic refers to this pattern as "a journey through chaos."[1] To be sure, many of the most enduring images of

American culture are those of movement, of journeys: immigrant ships sailing into Plymouth harbor, slave ships crossing the Atlantic, steamboats moving up the Mississippi River, frontiersmen trekking through the mountains, wagon trains rolling slowly over the great plains. As a people, Americans, Black and White alike, have placed great importance on this movement, according it the stature of a national myth. The image of a journey is, therefore, central to the American experience. The pattern of the journey takes shape in the first major Black autobiography, Gustavus Vassa's *The Interesting Narrative of the Life of Olaukah Equiano, or Gustavus Vassa, the African* (1789), and continues in the autobiographies of Hurston, Malcolm X, Anne Moody, and Angelou. Like the slave narrators who sought escape from bondage into a community that encouraged the development of self and fulfillment in a social role, these twentieth century autobiographers are also involved in a quest that will encourage the development of an authentic self. In a very real sense, Black American autobiography has its roots in the slave narratives that have helped to shape it.

The quest for recognition of one's individual identity is also a perennial theme in Black American autobiography. There is no age when a sensitive individual has not been troubled by questions concerning the meaning of his or her existence and his or her relation to the world around. Closely connected with the question of identity is the race issue. For the most part, however, Black autobiographers are individuals who have fought for and achieved their identity despite the efforts of others to deny them a sense of personal worth. The schism between what one thinks of oneself and what others expect one to be generates a special tension in Black autobiographical prose. Stephen Butterfield argues that the self of Black autobiography is generally not an individual with a private career, but a member of an oppressed social group with ties and allegiances to other members. Butterfield offers a profile of the traditional Black autobiography. He asserts that it is both a bid for freedom and an attempt to communicate to the White world what Whites have done to Blacks. Normally, Black autobiography is characterized by political awareness, empathy for suffering, knowledge of oppression, and a sense of shared life, shared triumph, and communal responsibility.[2]

To establish the place of Maya Angelou's autobiography in the tradition of Black American autobiography, one might suggest the following parallels. Like the accounts of Douglass, Baldwin, Malcolm X, Paul Robeson and Angela Davis, Angelou's autobiographical prose is characterized by political awareness, empathy for suffering, knowledge of oppression, and communal responsibility. Like Zora Neale Hurston, who creates a sense of the shared life she knew in Eatonville, Florida, as a Black child, Angelou recaptures the sense of life she came to know as a child in Stamps, Arkansas. While Hurston's technique for expressing this shared life is to speak in the village voice, Angelou's technique for expressing this shared life centers around the reconstruction of her childhood environment and the recapturing of her response to the environment. In her earliest work, she achieves this, in part, by remembering her past: the cotton pickers who came into her grandmother's store in the morning hours before work to buy sardines and cheese; the men and women who helped Momma to prepare the pork for sausage and who entered into the spirit of the revival and Sunday church services with joyful thanks and praise. Grandmother Henderson, Uncle Willie, Bailey, and the community at large are the center of Angelou's childhood and the shared life of that community is an important part of that childhood memory. As is obvious in the whole of her autobiography, Angelou, like Hurston, is concerned with Black life as it is informed and affected by the traditions and patterns of the past. And in common with the life of Hurston, the events in the autobiography are shaped by Angelou's command of the language, a level of articulation which employs both the linguistic rituals of the dominant culture and those of the Black vernacular tradition. For Angelou, the mission of autobiography is bound up with the spoken word and the oral tradition.

While it is true that the content of most Black autobiographies protest against social conditions, legal restrictions, and cultural traditions that have hindered Blacks, most often Black autobiographers achieve an effect of celebration in protest and affirmation in negation by describing the painful aspects of their experiences with humour and irony.[3] For example, Angelou's use of comic irony is one of the effective techniques of this tradition: Sister Monroe's "spirited" assault on the minister in *Caged Bird*, Angelou's stylish but inappropriate "get up" for her train trip from San Francisco to Los Angeles in *Gather Together,* the larger-than-life personalities who people her world in *Singin' and Swingin'*, the marvelously comic scene in *Heart of a Woman* in which her South African husband Vus Make chases Angelou around the lobby and up and down the elevators of a ritzy East Side New York hotel, and her leavening account in *Travelling Shoes* of the time she hires an African beautician to braid her hair "Ghanaian fashion," and the woman gives her a style similar to that worn by "pickaninnies" which Angelou mistakenly believes the beautician has done to teach her a lesson on the foolishness of trying to go native. Angelou's irony is not always derisive, as in her description of Mrs. Cullinan or her recapturing of the Mr. Red Leg's tale in *Caged Bird*. More often, as in *Gather Together, Singin' and Swingin', Heart of a*

Woman, and *Travelling Shoes,* she turns an irony of love and admiration on Black people with great effectiveness. The five volumes of the autobiography offer numerous excellent examples of Angelou's skillful use of comic irony in describing her relationships with people. A sympathetic irony in dealing with other Blacks has characterized some of the most outstanding work in the Black American literary tradition from Douglass' *Narrative,* to Ralph Ellison's *Invisible Man* and the work of more recent Black writers like William Melvin Kelley, Ishmael Reed, Toni Cade Bambara, and Toni Morrison.

However, Angelou's effective use of self-parody is something new in Black autobiography and, thus, creates a unique place in Black autobiographical tradition. Through numerous excellent examples of self-parody, in the first four volumes particularly, Angelou reveals her youthful silliness, her loneliness, her pretensions, her aspirations, and her instability. While most people encounter life, learn from experiences, and assume a more or less fixed set of postures toward reality, Angelou is unable to settle into security—not merely because life forces her to assume various roles, not merely because life whirls her along, but because, like the picaresque heroine, she is simply unable to keep to a set course. Angelou constantly lets go of the outer stability she sometimes finds because of the need for a vital tension between stability and instability. From the perspective of adulthood, she is able to parody this quality in her younger self for the purpose of analyzing that self. In doing so, she affirms the redemptive potential of all experience and the capacity of the individual human life to create meaning in the face of immense odds. Through the careful selection of actions and attitudes that lend to self-parody, Angelou is also able to reveal the genesis of her character and personality as she views her growth from the perch of adulthood.

Yet nothing in Angelou's prose—not even the parody of self—is merely humorous for the sake of laughter. Behind the laughter is a vision of human weakness, an empathy for people's foibles and their efforts to retain some semblance of dignity in the midst of the ridiculous. One of the values of Angelou's autobiography is to be found in the fact that from *Caged Bird* to *Travelling Shoes,* through all of the experiences recreated and the observations recorded, the work remains both sensitive and poised, humorous and empathetic, realistic and unembittered. How an understanding of the self leads to a feeling of kinship with humankind is excellently demonstrated in Angelou's autobiographical prose, particularly through her skillful use of comic irony and self-parody.

If Maya Angelou falls squarely within the Black autobiographical tradition because of the numerous parallels one discovers between her prose and that of other Black autobiographers, she also falls outside of the tradition because of the sharp differences between her autobiographical storytelling and others. Consider, for example, the childhood environments of Wright and Angelou. In their reconstruction of their environments, both provide moving accounts of their growing realization of what it meant to be Black in a White world. Equally important to their autobiographies is the unfolding of their own integrity of mind and the identity they create for themselves in order to survive and grow in a world that is structured to suppress their development. For example, as recorded in *Black Boy,* Wright is abused by family members for his independent spirit and is often made to feel like an unwanted outsider. He grows up in an environment that is characterized by fear, tension, and hostility. Wright places significant meaning in the suffering his family endures, exploring its repercussions into the deepest reaches of his own consciousness and linking its significance to his view in later years. In *Black Boy,* he recalls, "My mother's suffering grew into a symbol in my mind, gathering to itself all the poverty, the ignorance, the helplessness, the painful, baffling, hunger-ridden days and hours."[4] In contrast, Angelou grows up in an environment that is nurturing and supportive, an environment that includes the Store, tough but supportive relatives, the larger Black community. Wright discovers the power of books and language under circumstances reminiscent of the slave narrators. However, whatever the limitations of her segregated Arkansas school, that school and its teachers provide the young Maya the impetus for education and expose her to such writers as Dunbar, Johnson, DuBois, Hughes, as well as Kipling, Poe, Thackeray, and Shakespeare. Her autobiography reflects the urge to testify to the marvelous process by which her life has been shaped by books. Unlike Angelou, whose soul and spirit are also enriched by Black religious traditions, Wright, like many contemporary Black writers, has little use for the old-time religion. Although he is initially attracted to the stimulant religion provides for his imagination, belief never comes to him because he discovers a basic dichotomy between the realities the mind sees and the distortions of consciousness perpetrated in the name of religious truth. Even though Angelou is aware of this dichotomy, her belief in religion and the power of the word remains unshaken. Unlike the disintegration of community which takes place in *Black Boy* under the assault of Wright's questioning of the American dream, the cultural fabric of the Black community stands up to Angelou's probing analysis.

Anne Moody's *Coming of Age in Mississippi* (1968), published two years before *Caged Bird*, is a sensitively written book about Black youth coming of age during the Civil Rights movement of the 1960s and learning a new reality; yet the qualities of celebration and transcendence, so vivid in Angelou's autobiography, are missing. For example, before the end of the narrative, Moody is embittered and full of pessimism, her idealism having faded when the majority of poor Mississippi Blacks whose rights she has defended will neither support her nor register to vote. As she joins in the singing of "We Shall Overcome," the battle song of the Movement's foot soldiers, Moody concludes her autobiography with these words: "I wonder. I really wonder."[5] Unlike Angelou, whose innocence is somehow renewed with each bitter or bittersweet experience, by the end of *Coming of Age*, Moody is stripped of both innocence and faith.

The paucity of celebration and transcendence are even more evident in Mary Mebane's *Mary*. Throughout her autobiography, Angelou reminds us that she has come under the influence of some remarkable women: an upright and matriarchal grandmother; a glamorous, worldly-wise mother; several remarkable teachers in Arkansas and California; and numerous supportive, caring "sister friends." She gives generous credit to the combined influences of these women who serve as impressive role models. In contrast, Mebane grows into womanhood with no close friends and little support from her family, with the exception of her Aunt Jo, who gives her some small measure of love. While her mother gives the family what little stability it has, she is a distant, utterly unaffectionate woman. Mebane recalls that her mother remained cold and distant but that she herself never ceased trying to be good in order to win her mother's love. Ultimately, "This nightmarish relationship created a giant raw scar across [her] life."[6] Unlike the personal narratives of Wright, Moody, and Mebane, Angelou's autobiography affirms life itself, despite its difficulties, and celebrates the power of the individual to meet its challenges.

The strength which each volume of the autobiography characterizes bears witness to the fact that the positive aspects of life are empowering, because they enable the individual to surmount experiences of hardship or unhappiness. Although the protest-and-social-commentary theme runs through the whole body of Angelou's autobiography, a major theme embodied in the five volumes is not betrayal and disillusionment but rebirth and regeneration, the end of alienation, and the restoration to wholeness and community. Angelou's work asserts that although suffering may be extremely demoralizing and painful, it can have a regenerating effect on the sensitive, intelligent, and morally aware.

Maya Angelou's significance as an autobiographer rests upon her exceptional ability to narrate her life story as a human being and as a Black American woman in the twentieth century. In doing so, as one critic has observed, Angelou is performing for contemporary Black and White Americans many of the same functions that an escaped slave like Douglass performed for nineteenth century audiences through his autobiographical writings and lectures. This is say, both Douglass and Angelou function as articulators of the nature and validity of the collective heritage as they interpret the particulars of a culture for a wide audience of both Black and White Americans.[7] Moreover, Angelou illuminates the Black experience in an American context and in meaningful relation to the parallel and converging experiences of White Americans. In doing so, she provides her audience with a fuller realization of the Black

American consciousness within the larger context and demonstrates that, as people who have lived varied and vigorous lives, Black Americans embody the quintessential experiences of their race and culture.

Even though Angelou develops several prevailing themes in Black autobiographical writing (i.e., moving out and coming back, Black heritage as a source of regenerative strength, the role of elders in the Black community as mentors), her writing also contains other generally acknowledged universal themes. Among these are death and rebirth, movement from innocence to experience, idealism versus cynicism, the search for selfhood, and the importance of determining one's own self-definitions. Catholic in her sympathies, Angelou understands and regrets the suffering and misery not just of Black people but of humankind. Her coherent orchestration of these themes and her humorous, sometimes bitterly satiric portrayal of her creative life have established her as a significant voice.

An important literary artist is one who possesses significant ideas and feelings and who commands, as well, the technical ability to present those ideas and feelings effectively. Such an artist is Maya Angelou. Her artistry is demonstrated by her skillful techniques for presenting innocence, fledgling maturity, the contradictory selves of adolescence, and the centered focus of the adult woman; her striking and empathetic portraits of people; her powerful recreation of both the strengths and weaknesses in Black folk and cultural traditions; her gifted prose; the constant sense of color and warmth throughout the autobiography; her understanding of people; her amazing durability. One of the most memorable and unique characteristics of the autobiography is that it reveals a consistency in Angelou's vision of the human condition, particularly in the autobiographer's preoccupation with the effect of the community on the individual's achievement and retention of an integrated, acceptable self.

However, Maya Angelou's significance as an autobiographer is most apparent in the fact that her movement toward the interior self is constant throughout the five volumes of the autobiography, a movement which emphasizes its prominence as the central core of Angelou's values.

An Addendum: A Conversation with Maya Angelou

(I have chosen not to present an interview but to provide, through conversation, some insight into Maya Angelou's hopes for the autobiographical form.)

McPherson (hereafter designated as *DM*): I would like to follow up on our discussion of Lillian Hellman. I know that Lillian Hellman, in her autobiographies, does not speak as directly about herself as you do. That is to say, she speaks about those *others* whom she has come in contact with or with whom her life has been involved and, through these portraits of significant *others*, one is supposed to draw some image or truth about Hellman. I would like for you to speak to that or to take issue with it.

Angelou (hereafter designated as *MA*): I think that Hellman is a romantic and writes about things as she rather wishes them to have been. I see this in her writing about her childhood. I want to come back to that point because I don't know who does not, but I'll come back to that because I think that there's a difference. In writing about her childhood, she fancies herself much loved by the Black people who worked for her family and she does not see how complex that is, how that may not have been true at all; and if it was true (that she was loved by the cook and the Blacks who worked for her family) then those feelings are much more complex than she as an adult would appreciate. For her, these emotions are one-dimensional and that's what I mean by romantic. I don't mean it merely in just the sentimental sense, but romantic in a classical sense. She also writes about Lillian Hellman, the girl, as a one-dimensional character. For example, she says at one point that she developed a kind of rebellious nature due to the fact that she spent time with a grandmother in New York who was well-to-do and her mother was the poor daughter and she was the poor granddaughter. She says that in that moment, in that time, she developed a rebellious nature and a respect for people who had money. That's the only time I see any complexity in her confrontation with her retrospective memory of childhood.

DM: Let me ask you this question—What is the difference between her one-dimensional treatment of the Black cook and your one-dimensional treatment of Miss Gloria in her relationship to Mrs. Cullinan, because you don't address the complex issue behind her acceptance of that relationship.

MA: Good question. I think that I accepted Miss Gloria, the housekeeper, or rather showed the one-dimension of that housekeeper because I showed so many other dimensions of other housekeepers. It was as if one looks at one . . . if she was the only servant I dealt with in *Caged Bird* . . . then that would have shown that I also had that romance.

DM: What other servants do you deal with in *Caged Bird*?

MA: Well, the women who at once brought the clothes around to the house. The shirts and the things that they were ironing, the laundresses. . . .

DM: Where? The laundresses where? In Stamps? You seem to portray these women as Blacks in the community, as friends of Grandmother Henderson, but not as servants of Whites in Stamps. Except for Miss Gloria, we don't see them in that context.

MA: Yes, in Stamps. The ones who bring baskets of clothes around. I'll show you . . . it's there. The women whose hands were already roughened by the hard work but who learned to do tatting.

DM: Yes, you speak about tatting, but in terms of young girls, not in terms of these women as servants.

MA: Yes, young girls, young women.

DM: Young women who were taught to do tatting. I don't remember any other servant you portray in *Caged Bird*. Have I overlooked this?

MA: Well, I think Hellman only knew Black people who were servants in her home, but the servant class I deal with all through *Caged Bird*.

DM: The work class, but not the servant class. I believe there is a difference.

MA: The people who having worked all day would still get up to go to church, and then on the way home, there on the way home, their dissatisfaction, their questioning about life . . . how long will we be on the bottom, and in the church itself . . . not in the church, but in that tent. You see in the tent when the minister uses the sermon to talk against all Whites and the congregation is a mixture of cotton-pickers, housemaids, handymen, farmers, unem-

ployed and everybody agrees that though the Whites have
no charity and will not go to heaven . . . that is the point
of that particular episode: to show that in the total Black
community because all kinds of people are there from the
Black community and everybody's poor . . . the denomi-
national barriers are down so that the CME's, the Holy
Rollers, everybody is there. And everybody agrees—people get happy with the idea—that God hates the White people for their bad treatment of the Blacks and the chorus of
amens is unanimous. So I think that throughout I look at,
although there is this one incident of this housemaid, and
show the varying contradictions in the Black community—
in the servant class. You see what I mean?

DM: Yes, that's true in the Black community. But in
the direct relationship between the domestic servant and
White employer, it seems to me that Miss Hallelujah makes
a significant statement when she says, "Oh, she [referring
to the young Maya] broke *our* china" and that interjection
shows a strong identification with her White employer.

MA: There *is* that. I wouldn't have been telling the truth
had I not put in one person who had that attitude anyway,
but even that attitude is complex. Because while she felt
that way, and even as we know today, there are servants
and people who feel that way and who identify, it's much
more complex than that. You see what I mean; if I had not
had a Glory Hallelujah, this kind of woman, then the picture
of Stamps or of the time would not have been complete.
But while I have that, I also have this riding throughout the
work, a general malaise, and malaise is not a good word
for that, and the resistance through the church . . . the resistance through being good, etc. .

DM: But you speak of it, or it seems to me, that when
you deal with that, you are speaking of the irony that is a
part of the Black community and Black religion, just like

the irony that is apparent in the Joe Louis fight. I mean a victory that should be a reason for emotional joy is diminished by the reality of Stamps. The irony is that this Black man, though accepted in the boxing ring, the Black men of Stamps are afraid to go home that night because of the Nightriders. And the irony in the church scene, though these people can come out of the cotton fields bone-tired and drag themselves to the tent, and say amen to all of these things and really take joy in their poverty . . . take joy in their poverty and in their station . . . the irony is that nothing is really changed by religion; nothing is really changed by their active worship.

MA: Because they have to walk back. See, you saw the tent, where the tent was, over by the railroad tracks on this side of the pond. That was where all those (not all those but two or three) houses were and around where Miss Lizzy lived. So around that way, they could hear the records with the same music. . . .

DM: The same blues . . .

MA: I suppose in *Caged Bird* the White characters are as one-dimensional as Hellman's Black characters are. However, I do have a chance in *Caged Bird* to introduce the first White character who is more than one-dimensional. I begin to see this with Mrs. Kirwin. In the later books, the White characters take on flesh and contradictions and realities, something which is not true with Hellman. She continues throughout those works to see the Black characters as cardboard characters; so that's why I'm prepared to say that Hellman is a romantic when it comes to Black characters. Now if that is so, following that logic—it may not follow—but I tend then to look with a serious scrutiny at other aspects of her life which she describes. There is an incident in *Unfinished Woman* which is very telling to me. She has made for herself a hammock. She lives in a house with her mother, servants, father. It's a filled house, and she goes to school when she chooses. She says that she's so far behind when she goes up North that it's misery and so far ahead when she's down South that it's misery. But down South she can go to school when she likes and she takes her lunch and leaves and goes around to her hammock twice a week. In this one incident she spends all night in the hammock. She doesn't tell us anything other than that— that she slept all night in the hammock. I don't know what kind of family or servants would see a young girl out of the house all night . . . not check on her through the night at some point and have no remarks to make in the morning. It bothers me. She doesn't give us even a sentence after that. I'll show you. Here's a point, on page 14 of *Unfinished Woman*. Hellman is speaking of Sophronia who had worked for her parents: "She was a tall handsome light tan woman. I still have many pictures of the brooding face who was for me, as for so many other White southern children, the one and certain anchor so needed for the young years. So forgotten after that." I think that is just a line, but it substantiates my feeling of the romance, especially in that last phrase: "so forgotten after that." Because whatever romance of childhood's yearnings are involved in the relationship between the Black servant and the White child, it is unfortunate if that romance does not come under the scrutiny of the person as he or she grows; and I think this is the case in Hellman. Hellman still sees the Black, not only as a servant, but the Black person, I would think, as a one-dimensional character straight out of her childhood.

  DM: But isn't there some element of truth in that phrase—"so forgotten?"

  MA: That is the truth.

  DM: I mean some element of truth beyond her romanticism?

MA: But that's my point. That is the truth. She has told the absolute truth—so forgotten after that—but she doesn't go on then after she grows up to see the character as more. The servant is *not* completely forgotten. Obviously, she writes about the servant so he or she is not forgotten, and she continues to write even in *Pentimento*. She writes about the servant of whom she's afraid. The likelihood of Lillian Hellman being afraid of anyone is ludicrous. But still, the character, the Black character, the servant character, has crystallized for her in Sophonia, and I would imagine, in the other servants who worked for her or for her parents for the rest of her life.

DM: What point were you making about the hammock? I want to followup on it, your reference to the hammock.

MA: I can't find it. The point seems to me that a house filled with her mother, father, the boarders, her two aunts, the servants and so forth. I couldn't see how she would not be missed. A young girl growing up at that time . . . why there wouldn't be an alarm sounded if she stayed out of the house all night. So when I see that, it makes me think again about the kind of memory an autobiographer has and makes me question . . . it seemed to me to confirm my idea of the likelihood of a kind of a romance entering the telling of the story.

DM: Let me see if I can draw a parallel between that and what is for some readers a bothersome episode in *Caged Bird*. The car lot incident as you tell it. For one month you are able to be on your own. I'm not so concerned that your father makes no attempt to find you, but it seems to me so totally out of character that even if you were away from Vivian Baxter for a month that she would not have attempted to call you or to write you a letter; yet you are able to isolate yourself from the larger community, and nobody expresses concern . . . no one tries to find you.

MA: It's true. You might be able to draw the same parallel and it would be a good one because . . .

DM: And that is how the incident happened? Yours is an accurate retelling?

MA: Absolute.

DM: Numerous readers, including my students, have suggested that something must have been left out. The concern has been with how the autobiographer selects and focuses on his or her rendition of truth.

MA: I think that my recording of this experience comes from . . . this is going to sound very self-serving . . . but it comes from a kindness of my part in writing about Vivian Baxter. She was delighted that I was away, delighted . . . she didn't know what to do with me at that age.

DM: You were fifteen?

MA: I was fifteen. The year before, Bailey and I had been sent to Stamps as soon as school was out.

DM: That was the year after you and Bailey had returned to California.

MA: That's right. I had been sent back for the summer as soon as school was out. Mother got a pass from Daddy Jack, who had been her lover before Daddy Clidell and who was still on the railroad. She got passes for me and Bailey and sent us directly back to Stamps. Mama got a pass and sent us back.

DM: At the end of the summer?

MA: Yes. So when Daddy Bailey asked for me to come down to San Diego, she was delighted. It meant that she could run her house the way whe wanted without me around. I don't remember where Bailey went that summer, or where he was that summer. So her relief would keep her from calling; and possibly if she had called, Daddy would say that I was over at Aunt Estee's or over at Aunt Phyllis'.

DM: Or out with some friends.

MA: It's possible. Now if I had gone back with that scar, with that wound on my side, she would have questioned it and it would have given her a chance for some theatrics. She loved it—still does as you know—and my decision was at once to keep peace, but also not to give her that chance.

DM: Because you hated violence.

MA: I hated violence, but also I didn't want her to use me to get off. I disliked my father so much, but not so much that I wanted her to shoot him. So if I had never gone back, I don't know what would have happened. I mean . . .

DM: She would have been comfortable in her assumption that you were with your father.

MA: Unless Grandmother Henderson had asked. Grandmother Baxter didn't.

DM: So that's a kind of parallel situation . . . that and the Hellman episode.

MA: Yes, except that Hellman pictures her two aunts with whom they lived down there as being so loving and so supportive and her father loved her a lot.

DM: Yes, that certainly makes the difference.

MA: And right there in the house.

DM: At least you were out of sight.

MA: Yes, I was out of sight. I was six-hundred miles away and happily so for Mom. What I have left out of *Caged Bird* and all the books is a lot of unkindness.

DM: Of course. Morever, you were focusing on the development of your own maturity and insight.

MA: Because it is such a personal story, as opposed to a general story, I've never wanted to hurt anybody. So many of the people are still alive. The most difficult part for me has always been the selection of the incidents. To find one which is dramatic without being melodramatic or maudlin, and yet will give me that chance to show that aspect of human personality, of life which impacted on me from which I drew and grew. There are incidents during that period from thirteen to sixteen which I left out purposefully. It would not have advanced the story and would have hurt, would have destroyed someone. There are parallels in every autobiography despite the form the autobiography takes, that is whether it is diary or journal or memoir. What I have tried since *Caged Bird,* or maybe midway through *Caged Bird,* is a kind of storytelling in which it is true that I am the central character. But I suppose one of the reasons some of the readers ask, "Is that the Truth?," or that some critics probably think that I have novelized, fictionalized passages, stems from the fact that I see the incident in which I was a participant, and maybe the only participant, as drama . . . in the theatrical sense. And I've used, or tried to use, the form of the Black minister in storytelling so that each event I write about has a beginning, a middle, and an end. And I have tried to make the selections graduate so that each episode is a level, whether of narration or drama, well always dramatic, but a level of comprehension like a staircase.

DM: Like a level of insight, a level of maturity.

MA: That's right, I have tried.

DM: This is particularly so in *Caged Bird*—where you see that little girl, three years old, in the Prologue. It certainly is a step-by-step maturing or a step-by-step gaining of insight.

MA: If it is true in *Caged Bird,* I hope it is true in each book . . . also a level of broadening of vision. My ambition is vast for the autobiographical form and for me as a writer who uses the autobiographical form.

DM: What do you mean?

MA: Well, I would like to see autobiography in fifty

years. I would like to see writers use, really develop the autobiographical form.

DM: Writers have been developing the form since the seventeenth century. Develop it in what way? I don't understand what you're getting at.

MA: No, I don't think so. I think it's going some place. I'm aware that the novel as a form is new—it's only two or three hundred years old. And I think that autobiography could really be as . . . I have no idea where it's going, but I think that probably in another writer who comes from a totally different position could . . . well, I don't know if you saw a book called *Brother to a Dragon Fly*.

DM: No.

MA: It's an autobiography and the first three or four pages are so beautiful and so . . . the writing is excellent for one thing. The texture of the writing led me to think that the writer was going to explode the autobiographical form. I can't tell you what I mean . . . I have no idea what I'm talking about. But there may be another way of doing it.

DM: Of recreating one's history, of reporting one's suffering?

MA: Yes, and, of course, every writer writes autobiographically anyway, whether he's Eugene O'Neill or Arthur Miller or Paul Laurence Dunbar.

DM: My hope is not that the form will go in any particular direction, but that more scholars will begin to take the form more seriously; too many scholars either don't take autobiography seriously or they dismiss it summarily. Acceptance of autobiography as literature and cultural history is what I'm hoping for and this *is* what is happening in American Studies; there are enough people who have begun to accept autobiography, American autobiography especially, as a serious literary form.

MA:　As a serious art form.

DM:　As a serious art form, for both its literary value and its historical and cultural value.

MA:　I suppose that's what I'm really saying when I say that I have a great ambition for the form. It may have to make some qualitative jumps. I don't know; if it happens, it happens. I think it is maybe relevant that until I wrote *Caged Bird,* I had always considered myself a poet/playwright. So I brought to *Caged Bird* those two forms which I love a lot and which I had studied a lot on my own. So while Hellman is a playwright . . . maybe because she was so successful as a playwright . . . she didn't feel the need in either of her books to employ the playwright expertise or art for dramatic sake. Maybe because she was so successful. So she wrote her books, and her prose is not as informed in the dramatic sense, I think, as my episodic form which is almost like acts or scenes. My intention in the new book (*Traveling Shoes*) is to cut out editorializing altogether. I hope I can do it and tell the story of Africa by episodes, by scenes.

DM:　It seems to me that your editorializing and those comments that you encapsulate from certain episodes are what give your work its power and value.

MA:　Well, we'll see; if it doesn't work, it doesn't work. You remember that even in *Gather Together* I was going to try to include a fictional character. Anyway, I'm going to try and if it doesn't work, it won't work; I will go back to something else. But I'm going to try for something and if it works, it works. When one says that an autobiographer didn't have to use the autobiographical form for a particular work, I think that is true of all the autobiographers that you have been looking at, save Maxine Hong Kingston and me. Until *Tripmaster Monkey,* autobiography was Kingston's only art form. It is certainly my only prose form; although

I also use poetry too. But, my major platform *is* autobiography.

DM: Indeed, you *are* an autobiographer.

MA: Yes, that's what I am, so I have to use the form. Hellman had her plays and her screen plays before that. Dr DuBois had his essays and his political treatises—social and historical treatises, whether it was the *Suppression of the Slave Trade* or *Souls of Black Folks* or any of those other important treatises. He was not obliged to use autobiography in order to examine himself and his time. He had written enough other works. But Maxine Kingston, with *Chinamen* and even before that with *Woman Warrior,* and I are linked. We are the only ones I know who have made such extensive use of the form. It seems to me that in *Chinamen,* Maxine tried to expand the form. She did some wonderful things. It is a totally different book from *Woman Warrior,* but she is looking into the autobiographical form in an even deeper, strange way than in *Woman Warrior* though *Woman Warrior* is easier reading and rich. Yet I think the second book is more revolutionary as a form. She's really trying to get into whatever I was trying to say earlier. She's trying to make it work for her . . . to help her to examine herself, her time and other times through the autobiographical form because that's all she has. Whatever mistakes or whatever failures I have in my use of the form, I am still writing in the autobiographical form because I have no other. I just got a letter from Bob Loomis. Listen to this: "Dear Maya, how I wish now that I'd had a chance to read "The Reunion" [my short story] while I was down there. As you knew I would, I liked it a great deal." For Bob that's the epitome of . . . "And I particularly liked the way it was told. You seemed as at ease in that story as you are in autobiography, partly, I suppose, because it was told in the first person. The only plus in not reading the story there was now that I have the book I can keep it." But I am at ease in autobiography because it is *my* form. One of the best short stories I had written before "Reunion" was "Glass Rain." Again, in the first person. It seems to me that I lose contact when I get into fiction. I can write fiction, but I must write it from the first person. I lose contact when I put the third person singular in there. I cannot speak from the third person. I can't seem to. The first voices that impressed me for storytelling were the ministers', since I grew up in a household which was very quiet . . . Mama simply was very quiet . . . and then all those years I was very quiet . . . and the store was also quiet unless someone came . . . the radio didn't play. It played on Sunday morning.

DM: But not during the week?

MA: I'll tell you. It played on Sunday morning for us to hear "Wings Over Jordan;" in the evening it played around 6:30 to hear Gabriel Heater; if we had been very good, Mama would let us keep it on to hear "The Shadow" and "Gangbusters" . . . if we had been very good and she didn't have something else to do or didn't have her quilting bee over or something like that . . . then we could listen to "Gangbusters" or the "Lone Ranger" or "The Shadow Knows" or something like that. Other than that, it was quiet in the store. Mama occasionally would sing to herself, but there was very little talk. Mama would wash and braid my hair and go through all that without saying a word. She was not a talker.

DM: And your Uncle Willie didn't talk?

MA: No, he had the [speech] impediment.

DM: A prevailing silence.

MA: Very little conversation. First, Mama was not a gossip. If something had happened in the town and someone came to the store to tell Mama, she would say, "Umhum, Umhum. I see Sister Hudson," and then after she would leave, maybe Mama would say, "Did you hear that, Willie?" But otherwise, there was very, very little talk. So in the church, when the minister would make the Bible come alive . . . and I had decided to read the whole Bible . . . so when the minister would elaborate on the story, whether it was the Prodigal Son, or Dry Bones in the Valley, it would just go through the top of my head, Dolly. I could see it . . . and the tonality . . . and the old people . . . the music and all that. It was going to the opera for me.

DM: It was drama.

MA: It was high drama and I loved it so. So I never fought against going to church because I loved it. If there was a boring minister or something—but we had good ministers . . . even one who was a kind of itinerant minister who lived in the town and who drank, but he was really hot . . . so I loved church so. I think I loved the fact that Black minister said, "*I,*" "God told *me* personally." "*I* saw Jesus." You know, it was always the first person. The minister said, "*I* can see it now, down there in that valley; *I* see those bone, *I, I, I* always, so probably the . . .

DM: The *I,* the internalized "I;" that's a good point, I'm glad you brought that up. The personal narrative became a form for you.

MA: Absolutely.

DM: Let's move on. You telescope your period of voluntary mutism. How long a period did that extend? At one time, you said five years.

MA: Almost five years.

DM: From the time you were eight until you were thirteen?

MA: No, from the time I was about seven-and-a-half.

DM: You were raped when you were seven-and-a-half?

MA: Well, the rape took place months before I returned to Stamps.

DM: You had medical care, but you didn't have any other care.

MA: No, no psychiatric care. But Vivian Baxter simply could not . . . she didn't know what to do with me . . . well, in any case, she didn't know what to do with any child.

DM: Her sense of guilt also played a part, I suppose.

MA: I guess, that too. But also when she tried everything she could to bring me out, but what she had was dancing to bring me out and I could not respond to that.

DM: Well, you know I can't blame the Baxters too much because in the 1930s very few people understood about children who were traumatized by such incidents.

MA: She couldn't.

DM: And very few people had access to psychological care. There were no child psychologists in the schools at that time.

MA: I doubt it, and they wouldn't have thought to do that, I don't think. If they had known maybe.

DM: Now public schools have access to child psychologists. Today, a teacher would have told the family or the principal . . . somebody would have said, "She might need help," but schools didn't have such services in the 1930s.

MA: And psychological care would have suggested that I was crazy.

DM: Not that you'd been traumatized?

MA: I think that just before that, the rape incident, my grandfather had died.

DM: You don't talk about him. You have very little memory of him?

MA: I have no memory of him.

DM: But wasn't he living in the house when you and Bailey went to St. Louis?

MA: It seems so, but I have so little memory of him. I don't know if he died while I was there . . .

DM: Or before you came.

MA: No, I remember his accent, but I don't know how I remember his accent. I mean he may have been brought from the institution.

DM: What do you mean brought from an institution?

MA: He died in an insane asylum. And he was brought from the institution. Good Lord!

DM: You just remembered?

MA: Yes.

DM: How long had he been in the institution?

MA: I don't know.

DM: I can see now what you mean when you say your family would not have sought the help of a psychologist.

MA: He died in an insane asylum.

DM: Had he been there long?

MA: I don't know.

DM: I knew there had to be some reason why you didn't deal with him in *Caged Bird*. This is particularly striking because you use the people who come in and out of your life as mirrors which reflect *you,* the growing child.

MA: Yes, I know.

DM: The only thing you mention about him is his utterance, "Bah Jesus. I live for my wife, my children, and my dog." So your mutism lasted about four or five years?

MA: Yes. Now there were periods in that time . . . this is the first time that I'm thinking about that . . . but there were periods in that time. Until I was about twelve, I was pretty much silent. There were periods though . . . I'm trying to remember . . . when I would talk, but I can't remember why.

DM: Talk to people other than Grandmother Henderson, Bailey, and Uncle Willie?

MA: I don't remember. I can't remember, but there were periods when I would talk. I remember writing songs and I would teach them to Bailey. Goodness, I can't remember. I am trying to get back to that, but I think about songs. The kids would play ring games. When I'd play them, I wouldn't sing the songs with them, and they'd play on the hill going to school, on the path going up. Pop the whip and all those, but I would write songs. You know about that song "Julie?" Well, there was a game that the kids played. When I was in New York, say '68, I wrote a melody for Harry Belafonte, and since his wife's name is Julie, I decided to use that children's game which was (Maya singing melody and lyrics): "I call you Julie, before day, Julie; Julie would not answer, Julie; that's all right, Julie; that's all right, Julie." And I remember the kids playing the game in the evening around the store; it was a hide and seek game. So I called Bailey, in I guess in '67, or '68, to ask him what was the rest of the song and he said, "You mean you don't know? You wrote it and you taught it to me and I taught to the kids." I can't remember any of the others, but I remember standing at that side door . . . there used to be a back door . . . see there's a side door now, but there used to be a back door looking right out onto the garden and . . .

DM: It's been closed off, hasn't it?

MA: It has been closed.

DM: It looked like a new wall or something had been built. I examined the area, but I saw no evidence of where a door was.

MA: Yes, but there was a back door with a few steps going down.

DM: You know you refer to this in *Caged Bird;* and I couldn't get a sense of where the White children lived, or how they were coming down the hill. You remember that you were so upset . . that I didn't want to ask you. While I could imagine Grandmother Henderson on the front porch, I could not imagine the hill.

MA: Well, see straight out from the porch . . . now that's all grown over, but there was a path right across the street, right across that road, that big road.

DM: But the road was not so close then . . . the black top road?

MA: No, it was not as close then.

DM: The area was a yard and a part of your property?

MA: Yes, but there was an incline; well to me as a kid it looked like a hill. And there was a path straight up to the school. You could stand on the porch and see the school. Then there was a big oak tree just across the road and the path that went up like that to the school.

DM: Where did the White children live?

MA: They lived back over there around the cemetery, back behind that.

DM: That was some distance from the store.

MA: Oh, yes, but back over in there.

DM: That's where your grandmother had those houses. They lived on your grandmother's property.

MA: That's right; many of them lived on Mama's property.

DM: You still have that land now?

MA: Yes, I still own that, nothing but huts.

DM: You say the houses are nothing but huts now, but is it still your property?

MA: Yes. But there is something else about muteness which is just eluding me. I do remember that there were times when I would talk. I can't remember talking to any particular person other than Bailey.

DM: Did you talk to yourself?

MA: Maybe so. And I keep thinking of *Liberty;* there

was a magazine called *Liberty;* it cost ten cents and there were magazines like *Smith and Wesson;* but that was not the main one . . . a pulp paper magazine with short stories that cost ten cents. And I suppose the housekeepers and maids would bring *Saturday Evening Posts,* and there were short stories in them. And I don't know whether I read them aloud to myself, but I keep thinking of *Liberty,* in particular which was my favorite. I don't know whether I . . . can't remember. But it has something to do with *Liberty.* I don't know; but probably because I didn't talk, the language was so important, so important. And I formed a habit of listening, a habit which is still with me today.

DM: You don't say that Mrs. Flowers was a teacher although readers assume that. What was Mrs. Flowers?

MA: She didn't teach in Stamps.

DM: Why was she living in Stamps?

MA: Dolly, I don't know, but she didn't teach in Stamps.

DM: So why was she in Stamps?

MA: I don't know why; maybe she had a summer home in the town. I don't know, Dee, but she was so beyond everybody else, you know.

DM: Her summer voile dresses. . . .

MA: Oh, dear. She was about your color, maybe a little darker, and she had your skin.

DM: Another question about your family: Why didn't Uncle Lindsay help Lois with her college education?

MA: Because Lois wouldn't accept it.

DM: Would not accept his help in college?

MA: In college she wouldn't accept it. One of the reasons was that Lois had run away and married.

DM: Before she went to college?

MA: Maybe she ran away before entering college or she

dropped out of college. So when she decided to go back, she already had the kids and. . . . She might have come out of high school. I think she married at 19 or so. She may have been in college for one year and married against Uncle Lindsay's suggestion. The husband went on to school and is now either a dermatologist or an orthodontist.

DM: In Little Rock?

MA: Yes, in Little Rock. He lives in Little Rock. But the marriage had problems. When she left him she took Karen down to Stamps where she lived with uncle Willie. But that toughness is also there, especially in that Johnson side of the family, I guess. Also Lois's mother, Aunt Caruther, owns lots and lots and lots of property; and she is well off herself . . . I mean land rich. But Lois wouldn't accept help from any of them and did all sorts of things to support herself and children.

DM: There are so many questions. I am impressed by Uncle Willie who took in all those people, Lois, her children and others as well.

MA: All sorts of people. Also, Aunt Essie, who is my grandfather's daughter, not my grandmother's daughter, from Oklahoma . . . a Herndon. . . .

DM: Your grandfather left Grandmother Henderson and remarried?

MA: Yes, and had another family.

DM: Then ended up in San Bernardino?

MA: Yes, but my grandmother raised my grandfather's daughter from his second marriage.

DM: Yes, I saw that in her letter. There's a letter that she wrote after your father died. There's a letter in your papers that brings you up-to-date about your father.

MA: To take into your home and care for your ex-husband's child shows a particular kind of spirit.

DM: Indeed.

MA: After he had left her and married someone else and lived in another state, Aunt Essie came.

DM: And Grandmother Henderson took her by the hand and she, in turn, called her Mother Henderson.

MA: I think a parallel could be drawn between that and the African extended family . . . with the very wives calling their co-wives' children *their* children. And the fact that Nana Nketsia said that when he went to Tuskegee an anthropologist there told him that if he really wanted to see Africanisms, he should go to Stamps, Arkansas. And Nana had never known that I was from Stamps. I had never spoken to him about Stamps. There was no reason to. And especially at that time in Africa. Stamps was there with me, but it was so far away, although I kept feeling that I was in Stamps, which may be one of the reasons I could sense that I felt more at home in Ghana than I had ever felt in my life; I couldn't accept Stamps, but I could accept it in Ghana. But I never mentioned it, so when I told him in California that Stamps was my town, that Stamps was where I grew up and was formed, he thought I was kidding. He thought I was trying to latch onto something that he knew about. And I had nothing in 1965 or 1966 to prove that I really had grown up in Stamps. So he thought I was making it up. Then he would get angry with me and say, "You're not from Stamps." You know, that sort of thing.

DM: Did Vivian Baxter ever visit Stamps?

MA: Yes, she did go once.

DM: When?

MA: Before I was born. I think she went with Bailey in the arms.

DM: So that was her only visit until a few years ago; this meant that she never came while you and Bailey lived there, although Bailey Sr. did. But she wrote to Grandmother Henderson often, didn't she?

MA: Yes. I remember I wrote about that. I remember receiving a package of Christmas stuff from her.

DM: The tea set.

MA: Yes, the tea set.

DM: And the doll. That's a very moving passage, because it is your first confirmation of the fact that she's alive. Something else is also very interesting in your autobiography . . . Maxine Hong Kingston also does this in *Warrior Woman* . . . your use of fantasy. I don't know of any other autobiographers who use fantasy to define themselves as you and Kingston do.

MA: But children, particularly lonely children, always fantasize . . . always alter their reality through fantasy.

DM: That's true. My niece Jeanne used to have the biggest conversations with herself and create all kinds of playmates. She had a marvelous imagination.

MA: The same is true of Guy, who used to stand in the bathroom talking to seven or eight people. He also had a friend named Fluke. Whoever did something, it was always Fluke and Fluke was the one who made him do things. One day my mother said, "I'm tired of this damn Fluke. Where is he? I want to see him." Guy said, "He's sitting up there on the 'saladid'." So she said, "What's the 'saladid'?" He called the 'saladid' the valance; that was his name for it. "He's sitting up there on the 'saladid'." So my mother asked him, "How could be get up there?" She had those big-holed curtains, you know; when you pulled the drapes, there would be these cotton curtains, rather like eyelet. He said, "He puts his feet in those holes; he just climbs right up." I mean that whole way he used to tie up the chairs at night. The chairs were his horses and he would rope them.

When he'd go to bed he'd say, "I can't lie down just yet; I forgot to tie up the horses." Sometimes Mother's friends would come in and greet her, and start to sit down, and then Guy would say, "Don't sit down!"

DM: Don't sit on my horse?

MA: And these old people, old to me then, you know half-drunk, would look at Guy in amazement. I think that your seeing that about fantasy and having physically visited the town puts you in a position to know how I have tried to record my chilhood . . . also the fact of knowing what you know beyond what anybody else knows . . . for instance. Grandfather Baxter was not unlike James Baldwin's father.

DM: Yes, there is that similarity.

MA: Which in a strange way did for my family the same thing that Baldwin's father's illness did for the Baldwin family in that it drew them together, and it drew the Baxters together.

DM: And it forced Grandmother Baxter to be like iron.

MA: She had that already. But I think, though, that it did force them, the family, into a kind of rigid bond of loyalty which is the same thing; that is what happened with the Baldwins, so much so that people who marry into the family . . . this is fantastic . . . I hadn't thought of that. People who marry into the Baldwin family have a very rough time getting between those brothers and sisters. In the Baxter family, they are still the same; when I was growing up, Tommy was married to Della. They had been married for years, but when I would come into the house, or when anyone would come in, they would say, "All right, this is family talk now." And all the wives and husbands had to leave. In 1966, I took Miriam Makeba, the South African singer, to my uncle's house, really to Aunt Leah's house. Miriam was performing at UCLA and I took her there because it's very near, you know, five minutes from UCLA. So I took her around to visit the family with a friend of hers. It might have been Letta Mbula, the other South African singer, who accompanied us to Aunt Leah's house; Uncle Tommy was living there. We went in and my Aunt Della and everybody greeted us and gave us all soft drinks and everything; then Tom said. "Excuse me, we have to talk family"; he and I excused ourselves and went into the bathroom. He said, "How are you?" I said, "I'm fine." He said, "Everything all right?" I said, "Yes." He said, "You doing all right. Okay then, that's good." Then back out in the living room, he said, "We're finished with the family talk." So that kind of closeness, maybe fear and secrecy, drew the Baxter family together like a balled up fist.

DM: When did Mom move away from that, because she and Aunt Leah aren't close at all.

MA: Well, Aunt Leah. I don't want to get into that.

DM: Okay, but that was after Grandmother Baxter died?

MA: Well, Aunt Leah left home when she was about seventeen. She left St. Louis, branched out on her own and went, I think, with a fellow named Lavaleda Red, to the West Coast. That would have been in the late '20s, but all the fellows and Mom remained at home. I guess Mom came out in the thirties. I was born by that time, so it must have been 1929. I was born in St. Louis in 1928, but six months later—about October 1928—mother went out to Long Beach, California.

DM: Bailey has in a letter that he wrote to you, that someone told him that it was Grandmother Baxter who sent you to Stamps. He asks, "Do you know that Mr. Somebody said that it was Grandmother Baxter who sent us away?"

MA: Oh, yes, from California. But it wasn't she who

took us to the train; it was Bailey Johnson Sr. who took us to the train when we were three and four—Bailey Johnson Sr. took us to the train.

DM: I want to get this straight. Where was your mother?

MA: My mother was in Long Beach; Grandmother Baxter was also in Long Beach. My father took us to the train . . . he had a girlfriend. I think she rode part of the way with us. But what Bailey's talking about, I think, is that Grandmother Baxter is the one who would have suggested to my mother to let us go with our daddy. That is possible, but it was Bailey Johnson Sr. who put us on the train . . . he and his girlfriend. I think that there is a parallel to be drawn, probably between four people—DuBois, Hellman, Kingston and Angelou—only in the fact that *all* were very lonely children.

DM: Yes. Their very isolated childhoods provided opportunity for reflection and reading and for a kind of growth that other children normally don't have.

MA: I think also that another parallel that could be drawn between the four is that the circumstances, even though they were very different, were similar enough for rebellious natures to grow; in every instance, those four are rebellious. Now their demonstration of rebellion is very different. In my case, I just stopped talking.

DM: That's true. However, it is possible to see your cessation of talking as something else. I see it as growing out of confusion and guilt.

MA: Yes, that's true.

DM: But not necessarily rebellion. I see your beginning of rebellion . . . a kind of political rebellion, taking a stance . . . when you refuse to be addressed as Mary. However, your refusal to talk suggests something else to me.

MA: I'm sure you're right. I'm sure that what it started

from was the guilt and fear; you know, the muteness. I stopped talking for that reason. I think that it grows though; that sort of thing never remains just that . . . I mean that kind of psychological affliction.

DM: The kind that afflicts women, girl-children. I've talked with David Hill extensively about this phobia.

MA: Yes, but it grows to include other things.

DM: Would you have been rebelling against Vivian Baxter?

MA: It's possible.

DM: Were you rebelling against her casual involvements with lovers? You didn't understand the relationships then, but you were wise enough to know that something was involved. Also, you were involved with all of those Baxters.

MA: Yes, but I also knew that if I didn't talk I could withdraw from everybody. And only Mama, see, and Bailey . . . Oh Mama; Dolly, I can't tell you . . . that she would actually allow that. I was thinking about something . . .

DM: She allowed you not to talk.

MA: I was thinking about something in Canada yesterday, because I used Mama a lot in that speech, and I thought of something which I didn't talk about. I don't know if I wrote about Mama slapping the teacher. There was a teacher, a Miss Williams; I must have been about eight and Miss Williams had come to town. She was a little woman. I didn't talk in her class and she thought I was being impudent and I suppose (I didn't write about this?) I just wore her control down by not speaking. I would get up and write on the board. She slapped me and I ran out of the school, down the hill and right into the store with Mama crying. I told Mama that Miss Williams had slapped me. I don't remember if I wrote it, but I told Mama and my grandmother took off her apron in the front of the store, folded it, and put it across the candy counter. There wasn't anybody in the store. Uncle Willie wasn't there . . . so he may have been down at the house. Mama took the wooden board and we stepped out on the porch and Mama closed the door to the store and slipped the wooden board across the front. Then we walked up the hill. I stayed out in the yard, but Mama got Miss Williams and she came out in front of the school. My grandmother said, "Now that is my grandbaby; you are somebody's grandbaby;" (Maya slaps her hands to indicate her grandmother slapping Miss Williams). Just like that, and she then walked down the hill.

DM: That's marvelous.

MA: It wasn't recess, so there were no kids out.

DM: Grandmother Henderson, that gentle Christian lady.

MA: The only time I can remember my grandmother doing a thing like that. I can see her back going down that hill. I can see it. Isn't that something. And that's all she said: "That's my grandbaby, you're somebody else's."

DM: That has to be written. It's a marvelous story. What a strong, vital role model. She may not have always been able to protect her home from outside White forces, but she surely surrounded the household, her family, with a tough kind of strength and love.

MA: And to the extent that she could, she protected it from the law.

DM: Yes, she kept a decent relationship with the Sheriff so that he would come by when the KKK was on its rampages. She also kept a decent relationship with the White community so that even though Whites still felt they had an upper hand on her, she never lost her composure. The scene where she stands out in front of the store and never loses her dignity. She doesn't take her arms down, she doesn't unfold her arms, she doesn't look around; she just stands. She doesn't acknowledge the girls' presence nor does she acknowledge them as human beings. Instead, she treats them as nasty, rude children. Those early lessons, those early exposures are ingrained in the texture of wisdom Grandmother Henderson gave you.

MA: I told you what happened in Sweden when I sent for Mom during the shooting of *Georgia, Georgia*. You know how much trouble I was having with Diane Sands and all those people.

DM: Yes, I know the broad outline.

MA: When I first went to the Bay Area, I used to walk with my hands behind me like grandma did. I would do that and Mother, when I was thirteen, would come along behind me and pull my hands apart and say, "Stop walking like that; you walk like an old lady." Thirty years later almost, twenty-five years later, I had sublet the apartment in Sweden and I walked from location across town, just walking and thinking how was I going to hold the film together, get the music done and all that. I walked into the house . . . the place was on the third floor, so Mom could look down and see me coming. When I came in, she gave me a kiss and a drink and I went to the window. I was standing looking out at the park, trying to figure out what to do with all of the hostility. Mother came up and pulled my hands apart, in Sweden in 1971. I turned around and asked why and she said, "You look just like Grandmother Henderson." She said, "Whenever you rare back like that, put your hands behind your back, I know just what you are feeling." It reminded her of when I was thirteen.

DM: Like Grandmother Henderson going into herself.

MA: Yes. Let's go back to Kingston. In *Chinamen*, what Kingston tries is a kind of autobiography . . . I don't know if this even works . . . but a kind of autobiography in which she is not present. So that in 1970s she writes about the 1880s and, in a queer way, lets us see her background. It's a very strange form. That's what I meant in saying that she has experimented with the autobiographical form in such a way that she writes about a great-grandfather or grandfather and the uncles and the people in the village from which her parents came at the turn of the century and even before that, if I remember correctly. She lets us see the ethos, the hunger and the ambition of the villages and the villagers . . . their hopes in coming to Gold Mountain; it is as if *Chinamen* really preceded *Woman Warrior*. She continues to use fantasy, of course.

DM: I will have to look at her work more closely.

MA: I will too. It seems to me that even though Hellman intends to speak for an entire generation in all her work, in truth, she is speaking about a very small group. I intend to speak *about* a very small group, but in fact I also intend to speak *for* a very large community.

DM: Is that contradictory?

MA: That's an absolute contradiction. I never say that we all did this, but she does say this from time to time throughout her work. I remember a particular sentence, *that my generation,* but that may be true of a very small group of people. It wasn't true in Kansas; it wasn't true even in New York at the time.

DM: How can one presume to speak for a generation anyway.

MA: Especially when there was Willa Cather and Edna St. Vincent Millay and Faith Baldwin and Kay Boyle, who certainly were all concerned with other issues. Other people had much broader dreams and interests. So, I think, that is a particular difference. I think that while I write about myself and keep myself in the forefront of the story, I don't think I'm so self-centered as to think that I'm speaking for everybody. But on the other hand, if I told the truth, it is a truth about a time and an ethos in the national Black Community. I think Hellman tends to think that she speaks for a large percentage of the people, but never did because she was elitist from the very beginning.

DM: Poor, but an elite.

MA: Poor, but an elite. Absolutely, because she was White and, you know, fairly well off . . . well off enough to have somebody beneath her . . . I never did and didn't come from a people who had anybody beneath them, so to speak. There were people who were poorer than we, but that was just fate. I can never remember my grandmother looking down on anybody except people who were. . . .

DM: Good time people?

MA: Yes, good time folks. But they could still come and get a favor from Grandmother and run bills in the store just like anybody else. So there was nobody to lord it over. I think that remains true of Hellman when she went with Hammet, when she married and became a writer out in Hollywood and lived an elite life and became political: she never represented a large group of people and that I think is a salient point to be made about her and her work.

DM: Which is an important difference between you and Hellman. DuBois also speaks for a small intellectual group.

MA: Indeed.

DM: He wanted a larger audience and in time it became large but not during his lifetime . . . not during the time that he wrote or was involved in the action of history; although he speaks and writes as someone who is "inside history."

MA: And yet I think Kingston and I both share a similar *voice*. Kingston speaks personally, but she speaks for almost every Asian, every first-generation Asian-American.

DM: Unlike DuBois, who was always more concerned *about* history. He was very careful about placing himself inside history.

MA: I really think that the diversion of points in my work and Kingston's is a salient one.

DM: I agree. Lillian Hellman spends so much time talking about other people. Especially in the second volume.

MA: I'm going to spend some time this afternoon on *Pentimento*.

Notes

Notes to "Introduction"

[1] Roy Pascal, *Design and Truth in Autobiography* (Cambridge: Harvard University Press, 1960), p. 112.

[2] James Olney, "The Value of Autobiography for Comparative Studies: African vs. Western Autobiography," *Comparative Civilizations Review*, 2 (Spring 1979), p. 57.

[3] For an insightful discussion of the historical and literary characteristics of autobiography, see "Introduction," Stephen Butterfield, *Black Autobiography in America* (Amherst: University of Massachusetts Press, 1974), pp. 1–7.

[4] For a fuller discussion of this point, see Lord Butler, *The Difficult Art of Autobiography* (London: Oxford University Press, 1968), pp. 18–19.

[5] Sterling Brown, *The Negro in American Fiction* (Washington, D.C.: Associates in Negro Folk Education, 1937), p. 27.

[6] For an instructive discussion of the importance of the antebellum slave narrative, see Darwin T. Turner, "Uses of the Antebellum Slave Narrative in Collegiate Courses in Literature," *The Art of Slave Narrative,* ed. John Sekora and Darwin T. Turner (Macomb, Illinois: Western Illinois University Press, 1983), pp. 127–134.

[7] See James Olney, "Autos, Bios, Graphein: The Study of Autobiographical Literature," *South Atlantic Quarterly,* 77 (1978), pp. 113–123.

[8] Pascal, pp. 182–3.

[9] James Olney, "Autobiography and the Cultural Moment," *Autobiography: Essays Theoretical and Critical,* ed. James Olney (Princeton: Princeton University Press, 1980), p. 13.

[10] Mary E. Burger, "Black Autobiography—A Literature of Celebration," (Dissertation, Washington University, 1973), p. 183.

[11] As important as the autobiographical writings of Frederick Douglass, W.E.B. DuBois, Langston Hughes, James Baldwin and others may be to American literary, cultural, and socio-political history, the major impact of these writers on American culture is the result of their contributions in areas other than autobiography.

[12] See Patricia Meyer Spacks, "Stages of Self: Notes on Autobiography and the Life Cycle," *Boston University Journal*, 25, No. 2 (1977), pp. 7–17.

Notes to "Autobiography as an Evocation of the Spirit "

[1] Henry Thoreau, *Walden and Civil Disobedience,* ed. Sherman Paul (Boston: Houghton Mifflin, 1960), p. 1.

[2] George E. Kent, *Blackness and the Adventure of Western Culture* (Chicago: Third World Press, 1972), p. 188.

[3] From the Honorary Degree citation presented to Maya Angelou by Wake Forest University (Winston-Salem, North Carolina) at the May 1977 Commencement.

[4] Eudora Welty, *One Writer's Beginnings* (Cambridge: Harvard University Press, 1984), p. 34.

[5] Maya Angelou, Personal interview, July 30, 1981.

[6] Angelou, personal interview, July 30, 1981.

[7] Eugenia Collier develops this idea extensively in her discussion of James Baldwin's essays. See Collier's "Thematic Patterns in Baldwin's Essays," *James Baldwin: A Critical Evaluation,* ed. Therman B. O'Daniel (Washington: Howard University Press, 1971), pp. 134–140.

[8] Claudia Tate, Introduction, *Black Women Writers at Work*, (New York: Continuum, 1983), pp. xv–xxvi.

[9] Elmer P. Martin and Joanne Mitchell Martin, *The Black Extended Family* (Chicago: The University of Chicago Press, 1978), p. 1.

[10] Erik H. Erikson, *Identity: Youth and Crisis* (New York: W.W. Norton and Company, 1968), p. 16.

[11] See Liliane K. Arensberg's thought-provoking essay, "Death as Metaphor of Self in *I Know Why the Caged Bird Sings*," *CLA Journal*, 20 (December 1976), pp. 273–291.

[12] Maya Angelou, *I Know Why the Caged Bird Sings* (New York: Random House, 1969), p. 3.

[13] Ralph Ellison, *Shadow and Act* (New York: Signet Books, 1966), p. 23. In his essay on Richard Wright's *Black Boy,* Ellison associates the autobiography with the blues and asserts that, like the blues, it is an impulse to keep the painful details and episodes alive.

[14] Elizabeth Schultz, "To be Black and Blue: The Blues Genre in Black American Autobiography," *Kansas Quarterly,* 7 (Summer 1975), p. 86.

[15] Angelou, *Caged Bird,* p. 68.

[16] Elizabeth Schultz asserts that Black autobiography, like the traditional blues, expands the solo; the voice of the single individual singer retains the tone of the tribe. The blues autobiographer, by articulating the narrator's experiences—by lovingly absorbing these experiences in the narrator's consciousness—makes them comprehensible to the autobiographer and to those who listen to them.

[17] Arensberg, "Death as Metaphor," p. 277.

Notes to "Initiation and Self-Discovery "

[1] Maya Angelou, personal interview, December 5, 1984

[2] Robert A. Gross, "Growing up Black," *Newsweek,* 75 (March 1, 1970), p. 90.

[3] Edmund Fuller, "The Bookshelf: The Making of a Black Artist," *Wall Street Journal,* 16 April 1970, p. 16.

[4] Maya Angelou, *I Know Why the Caged Bird Sings* (New York: Random House, 1969), p. 3.

[5] Angelou, *Caged Bird,* p. 3.

[6] Angelou, *Caged Bird,* p. 4.

[7] Arensberg, "Death as Metaphor, p. 278.

[8] William H. Grier and Price M. Cobbs, *Black Rage* (New York: Basic Books, 1968), p. 49.

[9] Maya Angelou, letter to Rosa Guy, July 22, 1968, Maya Angelou Papers, Z. Smith Reynolds Library, Wake Forest University, Winston-Salem, North Carolina.

[10] Sidonie Ann Smith, "The Song of a Caged Bird: Maya Angelou's Quest after Self-Acceptance," *Southern Humanities Review,* 7 (1973), p. 368.

[11] Angelou, *Caged Bird,* p. 6.

[12] Angelou, *Caged Bird,* p. 7.

[13] Angelou, *Caged Bird*, p. 51.

[14] Angelou, *Caged Bird*, p. 42.

[15] Angelou, *Caged Bird*, pp. 50–51.

[16] Angelou, *Caged Bird*, p. 55.

[17] Angelou, *Caged Bird*, p. 8.

[18] Angelou, *Caged Bird*, p. 24.

[19] Angelou, *Caged Bird*, p. 46.

[20] Angelou, *Caged Bird*, p. 30.

[21] Angelou, *Caged Bird*, p. 31.

[22] Angelou, *Caged Bird*, p. 32.

[23] Butterfield, *Black Autobiography*, pp. 211–212.

[24] Angelou, *Caged Bird*, p. 110.

[25] Angelou, *Caged Bird*, p. 9.

[26] Angelou, *Caged Bird*, p. 9.

[27] Angelou, *Caged Bird*, pp. 9–10.

[28] Angelou, *Caged Bird*, pp. 23–24.

[29] See Elizabeth A. Schultz's discussion of this point in "The Insistence Upon Community in the Contemporary Afro-American Novel," *College English*, 41.2 (October 1979), pp. 170–184.

[30] Angelou, *Caged Bird*, p. 133.

[31] Angelou, *Caged Bird*, p. 134.

[32] Angelou, *Caged Bird*, p. 135.

[33] Angelou, *Caged Bird*, pp. 134–135.

[34] Dr. Lindsay Johnson, personal interview, June 16, 1983.

[35] Angelou, *Caged Bird*, p. 53.

[36] See Donald B. Gibson, "Individualism and Community in Black History and Fiction," *Black American Literature Forum*, 9.4 (Winter 1977), pp. 123–129.

[37] Angelou, *Caged Bird*, p. 68.

[38] Angelou, *Caged Bird*, p. 68.

[39] Angelou, *Caged Bird*, p. 71.

[40] Angelou, *Caged Bird*, pp. 82–83.

[41] Angelou, *Caged Bird*, p. 85.

[42] Angelou, *Caged Bird*, p. 86.

[43] Angelou, *Caged Bird*, p. 86.

[44] Angelou, *Caged Bird*, p. 91.

[45] Angelou, *Caged Bird*, p. 92.

[46] Maya Angelou, scrapbook compiled during school year 1936–37, Maya Angelou Papers, Z. Smith Reynolds Library, Wake Forest University, Winston-Salem, North Carolina.

[47] Angelou, *Caged Bird*, p. 106.

⁴⁸ For a fuller discussion of this idea, see Selwyn R. Cudjoe, "Maya Angelou and the Autobiographical Statement," in *Black Women Writers (1950–1980)*, ed. Mari Evans (New York: Doubleday, 1984), pp. 12–14.

⁴⁹ Angelou, *Caged Bird*, p. 127.

⁵⁰ Angelou, *Caged Bird*, p. 128.

⁵¹ Angelou, *Caged Bird*, p. 128.

⁵² Sidonie Smith, *Where I'm Bound: Patterns of Slavery and Freedom in Black American Autobiography* (Westport, Connecticut: Greenwood Press, 1974), p. 130.

⁵³ Angelou, *Caged Bird*, pp. 131–132.

⁵⁴ Angelou, *Caged Bird*, p. 176.

⁵⁵ Elizabeth Schultz, "To Be Black and Blue," p. 88.

⁵⁶ Angelou, *Caged Bird*, pp. 179–180.

⁵⁷ Angelou, *Caged Bird*, p. 184.

⁵⁸ Angelou, *Caged Bird*, p. 203.

⁵⁹ Angelou, *Caged Bird*, p. 205.

⁶⁰ Angelou, *Caged Bird*, p. 206.

⁶¹ Angelou, *Caged Bird*, pp. 213–214.

⁶² Angelou, *Caged Bird*, p. 219.

⁶³ Angelou, *Caged Bird*, p. 218.

⁶⁴ Angelou, *Caged Bird*, p. 219.

⁶⁵ Angelou, *Caged Bird*, p. 232.

⁶⁶ Angelou, *Caged Bird*, p. 247.

⁶⁷ Angelou, *Caged Bird*, p. 247.

⁶⁸ Angelou, *Caged Bird*, p. 247.

⁶⁹ Angelou, *Caged Bird*, p. 267.

⁷⁰ Angelou, *Caged Bird*, pp. 272–273.

⁷¹ Angelou, *Caged Bird*, p. 281.

⁷² Smith, *Where I'm Bound*, p. 134.

⁷³ Angelou, *Caged Bird*, p. 264.

Notes to "The Contradictory and Imaginative Selves"

¹ Karl Weintraub, "Autobiography and Historical Consciousness," *Critical Inquiry* 1 (1975), p. 833.

² Wayne Warga, "Maya Angelou: One-Woman Creativity Cult," *Los Angeles Times*, California Section, January 9, 1972, p. 1.

[3] Maya Angelou, *Gather Together in My Name* (New York: Random House, 1974), pp. 65–66.

[4] Angelou, *Gather Together*, p. 73.

[5] Angelou, *Gather Together*, p. 81.

[6] Angelou, *Gather Together*, p. 170.

[7] Angelou, *Gather Together*, p. 194.

[8] Angelou, *Gather Together*, p. 3.

[9] Angelou, *Gather Together*, p. 4.

[10] Angelou, *Gather Together*, p. 5.

[11] Angelou, *Gather Together*, p. 6.

[12] Angelou, *Gather Together*, p. 61.

[13] Angelou, *Gather Together*, p. 211.

[14] See George E. Kent, "Maya Angelou's *I Know Why the Caged Bird Sings* and Black Autobiographical Tradition," *Kansas Quarterly*, 7 (Summer 1975), pp. 72–78.

[15] Angelou, *Gather Together*, pp. 5–6.

[16] Angelou, *Gather Together*, p. 8.

[17] Angelou, *Gather Together*, p. 34.

[18] Angelou, *Gather Together*, p. 7.

[19] Angelou, *Gather Together*, pp. 35–37.

[20] Angelou, *Gather Together*, p. 74.

[21] Angelou, *Gather Together*, p. 94.

[22] Angelou, *Gather Together*, p. 181.

[23] Angelou, *Gather Together*, p. 181.

[24] Roy Pascal, *Design and Truth in Autobiography* (Cambridge: Harvard University Press, 1960), p. 195.

[25] Angelou, *Gather Together*, p. 31.

[26] Angelou, *Gather Together*, pp. 116–117.

[27] Angelou, *Gather Together*, pp. 85–86.

[28] Angelou, *Gather Together*, p. 23.

[29] Angelou, *Gather Together*, p. 21.

[30] Angelou, *Gather Together*, p. 29.

[31] Angelou, *Gather Together*, p. 67.

[32] Angelou, *Gather Together*, p. 35.

[33] Tate, *Black Women Writers*, pp. xv–xxvi.

Notes to "The Adult Self in Bloom "

[1] See L. Joseph Stone and Joseph Church, *Childhood and Adolescence* (New York: Random House, 1957), pp. 334–335.

[2] Maya Angelou, *Singin' and Swingin' and Gettin' Merry Like Christmas* (New York: Random House, 1976), p. 20.

[3] Angelou, *Singin' and Swingin'*, p. 28.

[4] Angelou, *Singin' and Swingin'*, p. 35.

[5] Angelou, *Singin' and Swingin'*, p. 44.

[6] Angelou, *Singin' and Swingin'*, p. 85.

[7] Angelou, *Singin' and Swingin'*, p. 85.

[8] Angelou, *Singin' and Swingin'*, p. 31.

[9] Angelou, *Singin' and Swingin'*, p. 156.

[10] Angelou, *Singin' and Swingin'*, p. 153.

[11] Angelou, *Singin' and Swingin'*, pp. 184–185.

[12] Angelou, *Singin' and Swingin'*, pp. 189–190.

[13] Angelou, *Singin' and Swingin'*, p. 232.

[14] Angelou, *Singin' and Swingin'*, p. 147.

[15] Maya Angelou, *The Heart of a Woman* (New York: Random House, 1981), p. 3.

[16] Angelou, *Heart*, p. 3.

[17] Angelou, *Heart*, p. 46.

[18] Angelou, *Heart*, pp. 46–47.

[19] Angelou, *Heart*, pp. 44–45.

[20] Angelou, *Heart*, p. 93.

[21] Angelou, *Heart*, p. 169

[22] Angelou, *Heart*, p. 170.

[23] Maya Angelou, personal interview, October 11, 1981.

[24] Angelou, *Heart*, pp. 179–180.

[25] Angelou, *Heart*, p. 195.

[26] Angelou, *Heart*, p 197.

[27] Maya Angelou, personal interview, October 11, 1981.

[28] Angelou, *Heart*, p. 141.

[29] Angelou, *Heart*, p. 247.

[30] Angelou, *Heart*, p. 257.

[31] Angelou, *Heart*, p. 257.

[32] Angelou, *Heart*, p. 128.

Notes to "Redefining the Self Through Place and Culture"

[1] Butterfield, *Black Autobiography*, p. 3.

[2] See Thomas Neumann, "Maya Angelou in Search of Roots: Sojourn to Ghana," *Houston Chronicle*, 13 July 1986, p. 17.

[3] See Harold A. Issacs, *The New World of Negro Americans* (New York: Viking Compass Edition, Fifth Printing, 1969), pp. 288–305.

[4] Maya Angelou, *All God's Children Need Traveling Shoes* (New York: Random House, 1986), pp. 10–11.

[5] Angelou, *Traveling Shoes*, p. 12.

[6] Angelou, *Traveling Shoes*, p. 12.

[7] Angelou, *Traveling Shoes*, p. 19.

[8] Angelou, *Traveling Shoes*, p. 21.

[9] Angelou, *Traveling Shoes*, pp. 20–21.

[10] I am indebted to Barbara T. Christian's insightful article, "Maya Angelou's African Sojourn Links Two Worlds," *The Chicago Tribune*, 23 March 1986, Section 14, p. 35.

[11] Angelou, *Traveling Shoes*, p. 73.

[12] Angelou, *Traveling Shoes*, p. 73.

[13] Angelou, *Traveling Shoes*, pp. 73–74.

[14] Angelou, *Traveling Shoes*, p. 74.

[15] Angelou, *Traveling Shoes*, p. 76.

[16] Angelou, *Traveling Shoes*, p. 52.

[17] Angelou, *Traveling Shoes*, p. 85.

[18] Angelou, *Traveling Shoes*, p. 155.

[19] Angelou, *Traveling Shoes*, p. 35.

[20] Angelou, *Traveling Shoes*, p. 173.

[21] Angelou, *Traveling Shoes*, pp. 127–128.

[22] Angelou, *Traveling Shoes*, pp. 124,125.

[23] Angelou, *Traveling Shoes*, p. 128.

[24] Angelou, *Traveling Shoes*, p. 130.

[25] Angelou, *Traveling Shoes*, p. 130.

[26] Angelou, *Traveling Shoes*, p. 130.

[27] Angelou, *Traveling Shoes*, p. 145.

[28] Letter dated January 15, 1965, from Malcolm X to Maya Angelou, Maya Angelou Papers, Z. Smith Reynolds Library, Wake Forest University, Winston-Salem, North Carolina.

[29] Angelou, *Traveling Shoes*, p. 196.

Notes to "The Significance of Maya Angelou in Black Autobiographical Tradition"

[1] See George E. Kent, "Maya Angelou's *I Know Why the Caged Bird Sings* and Black Autobiographical Tradition," Kansas Quarterly, 7 (Summer 1975), pp. 72–78.

² For a fuller discussion of the historical and literary characteristics of Black autobiography, see Introduction to Butterfield's *Black Autobiography,* pp. 1–7.

³ Mary W. Burger develops this point extensively in "Black Autobiography—A Literature of Celebration," (Dissertation, Washington University, 1973), p. 27.

⁴ Richard Wright, *Black Boy* Perennial Classic (New York: Harper and Row, 1966), p. 111.

⁵ Anne Moody, *Coming of Age in Mississippi* (New York: The Dial Press, 1968), p. 348.

⁶ Mary E. Mebane, *Mary* (New York: The Viking Press, 1981), p. 28.

⁷ I am indebted to Lynn Z. Bloom for her excellent critical assessment of Maya Angelou in Volume 8 of the *Dictionary of Literary Biography*.

Bibliography of Works Cited

Angelou, Maya. *I Know Why the Caged Bird Sings*. New York: Random House, 1970.

—. *Gather Together in My Name*. New York: Random House, 1974.

—. *Singin' and Swingin' and Gettin' Merry Like Christmas.* New York: Random House, 1976.

—. *The Heart of a Woman*. New York: Random House, 1980.

—. *All God's Children Need Traveling Shoes*. New York: Random House, 1986.

—. Personal Correspondence, 1931–1940, Maya Angelou Papers, Rare Books Collection, Z. Smith Reynolds Library, Wake Forest University, Winston-Salem, North Carolina.

Mebane, Mary E. *Mary*. New York: The Viking Press, 1981.

Moody, Anne. *Coming of Age in Mississippi*. New York: The Dial Press, 1968.

Thoreau, Henry, *Walden and Civil Disobedience*, ed. Paul Sherman. Boston: Houghton Mifflin Riverside Editions, 1957, 1960.

Transcripts of Taped Conversations. Maya Angelou, Lindsay Johnson, Dolly A. McPherson, 1980–1985.

Welty, Eudora. *One Writer's Beginnings*. Cambridge: Harvard University Press, 1984.

Wright, Richard. *Black Boy*. New York: Harper and Row Perennial Classic, 1966.

Theory and Criticism of Autobiography

Arensberg, Lilliane K. "Death as Metaphor of Self in *I Know Why the Caged Bird Sings*." *CLA Journal*, 20 (December 1976), 273–291.

Baker, Houston A., Jr. "The Problem of Being: Some Reflections on Black Autobiography." *Obsidion*, 1 (Spring 1975), 18–35.

—. *The Journey Back: Issues in Black Literature and Criticism*. Chicago: The University of Chicago Press, 1980.

Barton, Rebecca C. *Witnesses for Freedom: Negro Americans in Autobiography*. New York: Harper, 1948.

Blackburn, Regina Lynn. "Conscious Agents of Time and Self: The Lives and Styles of African-American Women as Seen Through Their Autobiographical Writings." Dissertation, The University of New Mexico, 1978.

Blassingame, John. "Black Autobiographies as History and Literature." *The Black Scholar 5* (December 1973–January 1974), 2–9.

Burger, Mary W. "Black Autobiography—A Literature of Celebration." Dissertation, Washington University, 1973.

Butler, Richard Austen. *The Difficult Art of Autobiography*. Oxford: The Clarendon Press, 1968.

Butterfield, Stephen. *Black Autobiography in America*. Amherst: University of Massachusetts Press, 1974.

Couser, G. Thomas. "The Shape of Death in American Autobiography." *Hudson Review* 31 (1978), 53–66.

Cudjoe, Selwyn. "Maya Angelou and the Autobiographical Statement," in *Black Women Writers* (1950–1980), ed. Mari Evans (New York: Doubleday, 1984), 12–14.

Foster, Frances Smith. *Witnessing Slavery: The Development of Ante-Bellum Slave Narrative*. Westport, Connecticut: Greenwood Press, 1979.

Fuller, Edmund. "The Bookshelf: The Making of a Black Artist. *Wall Street Journal*, 16 April 1970, 16.

Jelinek, Estelle C., ed. *Women's Autobiography: Essays in Criticism*. Bloomington: Indiana University Press, 1980.

Kent, George E. "Maya Angelou's *I Know Why the Caged Bird Sings* and Black Autobiographical Tradition." *Kansas Quarterly*, 7 (Summer 1975), 72–78.

Olney, James. "Autos., Bios. Biographies, Graphein: The Study of Autobiographical Literature." *South Atlantic Quarterly*, 77 (1978), 113–123.

—. "Autobiography and the Cultural Moment." *Autobiography: Essays, Theoretical and Critical*, ed. James Olney (Princeton: Princeton University Press, 1980), 13.

—. *Metaphors of Self: The Meaning of Autobiography*. Princeton: Princeton University Press, 1972.

Pascal, Roy. *Design and Truth in Autobiography*. Cambridge: Harvard University Press, 1960.

Porter, Roger and H.R. Wolf. *The Voice Within: Reading and Writing Autobiography*. New York: Knopf, 1973.

Rosenblatt, Roger. "Black Autobiography: Life as the Death Weapon." *Au-*

tobiography: Essays Theoretical and Critical, ed. James Olney. Princeton: Princeton University Press, 1980, 47–54.

Sayre, Robert F. "The Proper Study—Autobiographies in American Studies." *American Quarterly* 29.3 (1977), 241–262.

Schultz, Elizabeth. "To Be Black and Blue: The Blues Genre in Black American Autobiography." *Kansas Quarterly,* 7 (Summer 1975), 81–96.

Sekora, John and Darwin T. Turner, eds. *The Art of the Slave Narrative.* Macomb, Illinois: Western Illinois University Press, 1983.

Smith, Sidonie Ann. "The Song of a Caged Bird: Maya Angelou's Quest After Self-Acceptance." *Southern Humanities Review,* 7 (1973), 368–375.

—. *Where I'm Bound: Patterns of Slavery and Freedom in Black American Autobiography.* Westport, Connecticut: Greenwood Press, 1974.

Smith, Henry Nash. "Can American Studies Develop a Method?" *American Quarterly* 9.2 (Summer 1957), 97–108.

Spacks, Patricia Meyer. "Women's Stories, Women's Selves." *Hudson Review,* 30 (1977), 29–46.

—. "Stages of Self: Notes on Autobiography and the Life Cycle." *Boston University Journal* 25.2 (1977), 7–17.

Stone, Albert E. "Autobiography and American Culture," *American Studies: An International Newsletter,* 11, No. 2 (Winter 1972), 22–36.

—. "Patterns in Recent Black Autobiography." *Phylon,* 39.1 (March 1978), 18–34.

Tate, Claudia, ed. *Black Women Writers at Work.* New York: Continuum, 1983.

Weintraub, Karl Joachim. *The Value of the Individual Self and Circumstance in Autobiography.* Chicago: University of Chicago Press, 1978.

—. "Autobiography and Historical Consciousness." *Critical Inquiry,* 1 (1975), 833.

Warga, Wayne. "Maya Angelou: One-Woman Creativity Cult," *Los Angeles Times,* 9 January, 1972, California Magazine.

Other Works

Billingsley, Andrew. *Black Families in White America.* Englewood Cliffs: Prentice-Hall, Inc. 1968.

—. *Black Families and the Struggle for Survival.* New York: Friendship Press, 1974.

Brown, Sterling. *The Negro in American Fiction.* Washington, D.C.: Associates in Negro Folk Education, 1937.

Collier, Eugenia. "Thematic Patterns in Baldwin's Essays," *James Baldwin: A Critical Evaluation,* ed. Therman B. O'Daniel. Washington, D.C.: Howard University Press, 1977.

Davis, Angela. "Reflections on the Black Woman's Role in The Community of Slaves." *Black Scholar*, 3 (December 1971), 2–16.

Ellison, Ralph. *Shadow and Act*. New York: Random House, 1964.

Erikson, Erik H. *Childhood and Society*. New York: W.W. Norton and Co., 1963.

—. *Identity: Youth and Crisis*. New York: W.W. Norton and Co., 1968.

—. *Life History and the Historical Moment*. New York: W.W. Norton and Co., 1975.

Gibson, Donald B. "Individualism and Community in Black History and Fiction." *Black American Literature Forum*, 11 (Winter 1977), 123–129.

Grier, William and Price Cobb. *Black Rage*. New York: Basic Books, 1968.

Kearns, Francis E., ed. *The Black Experience*. New York: The Viking Press, 1961.

Kent, George E. *Blackness and the Adventure of Western Culture*. Chicago: Third World Press, 1972.

Levine, Lawrence W. *Black Culture and Black Consciousness*. New York: Oxford University Press, 1977.

Mays, Benjamin E. *The Negro's God as Reflected in His Literature*. New York: Russell and Russell, 1968.

Staples, Robert, ed. *The Black Family*. Belmont, California; Wadsworth Publishing Co., 1971.

—. *The Black Woman in America: Sex, Marriage and the Family*. Chicago: Nelson Hall Publishers, 1973.

Stone, Joseph L. and Joseph Church. *Childhood and Adolescence*. New York: Random House, 1957.

Also published by Virago

The Autobiographical Works of Maya Angelou

'Not since the days of my childhood, when people in books were more real than the people one saw every day, have I found myself so moved' – *James Baldwin*

I Know Why the Caged Bird Sings

A powerful evocation of her childhood years in the thirties. In Stamps, Arkansas, Maya Angelou learns the power of 'whitefolk' at the other end of town, and suffers the trauma of rape by her mother's lover.

Gather Together in My Name

Maya Angelou is a young mother in California, unemployed, isolated, embarking on brief affairs and transient jobs. Burdened by family drama and racial bigotry, she turns to prostitution and narcotics.

Singin' and Swingin' and Gettin' Merry Like Christmas

Music and her son are the focus of Maya Angelou's life. She is on the edge of a new world; marriage, showbusiness and in 1954, a triumphant tour of 'Porgy and Bess'.

The Heart of a Woman

Maya Angelou becomes immersed in the world of Black writers and artists in Harlem, working in the civil rights movement with Martin Luther King.

All God's Children Need Travelling Shoes

Emigration to Ghana – where Maya Angelou comes to a new awareness of love, friendship and motherhood, civil rights and slavery – and the myth of mother Africa.

The Poetry of Maya Angelou

'Maya Angelou writes from the heart and her language rings clear and true . . . Whether joyful, sad or playful, her poems speak with delicacy and depth of feeling' – *Publishers Weekly*

'Maya Angelou liberates and exhilarates through her magical, lyrical, mystical medium – poetry' – *Mary Bryce, Tribune*

And Still I Rise

Maya Angelou's poetry – lyrical and dramatic, exuberant and playful – speaks of love, longing, partings; of freedom and of shattered dreams.

Now Sheba Sings the Song (with Art by Tom Feelings)

In this beautiful book Maya Angelou's poetry is complemented by the beautiful work of the Black American artist Tom Feelings. His portraits of Black women, drawn from life over a period of twenty years, are the context for the poet's sensuous verse.

Just Give Me ? Cool Drink of Water 'Fore I Diiie

In this marvellous collection, tender poems of longing, wry glances at betrayal and isolation combine with a fierce insight into 'hate and hateful wrath' in an unforgettable picture of the hopes and concerns of one of America's finest contemporary Black writers.

I Shall Not Be Moved

In her newest collection of verse, Maya Angelou winds skeins of desire and longing; throws punches – some tough, some tender; flaunts and beguiles – and pokes fun. With a new bittersweet mellowness, she sings the pleasures and pains of ageing.